DIFFICULT DECIS
IN 90 ⸲ Swi
ʰat

For a complete list of Management Books 2000 titles
visit our web-site on http://www.mb2000.com

DIFFICULT DECISIONS SOLVED

Patrick Forsyth

Copyright © Patrick Forsyth 2009

First published in 2009 by Management Books 2000 Ltd
Forge House, Limes Road
Kemble, Cirencester
Gloucestershire, GL7 6AD, UK
Tel: 0044 (0) 1285 771441
Fax: 0044 (0) 1285 771055
Email: info@mb2000.com
Web: www.mb2000.com

British Library Cataloguing in Publication Data is available

ISBN 9781852526139

I have yet to see any problem, however complicated, which looked at in the right way, did not become still more complicated.

Poul Anderson

Contents

1

Introduction:
Some important realities

Men do not stumble over mountains,
they stumble over molehills.

Confucius

Management was perhaps never easy; in the modern workplace it can be a downright struggle. Saying so does not, of itself, make it any easier for the hard-pressed manager to succeed. Managing people, and ensuring planned results are achieved, is a complex process. But certain approaches are key to it being made a success. There is plenty of advice around which sets out to make the process easier.

Despite this, you may be forgiven for saying that it is a tough job. Two things are prime in conspiring to make this true. First, management is a complex process. This is true both in the sense that many things that must be done are themselves complex, and in the sense that there are normally many different things to be done, often in parallel. Secondly, the work environment in which things must be done is hectic. Many people might say that it is increasingly hectic and that hectic understates the situation.

Certainly many managers work under pressure and, though some of this is good and stimulates performance, too much can

9

compound the difficulty of any job and have a negative effect. Lack of time, limited resources, impossible deadlines, overwhelming administrative detail and ever-changing technology – all this and more add to the pressure on those working in the modern workplace, and the stress that can accompany it.

I try to take one day at a time, but sometimes several days attack me at once.

Graffiti

You are doubtless a manager of some competence (or you would surely not be reading this book). You utilise your experience (however brief to date), and certainly you achieve things (or you would be out on your ear). You work to make this possible too, keeping up to date, extending and refining your skills, and thinking before you act (though you may feel pressure of time curtails this to some extent).

But do you achieve – or even get done – as much as you want? Even the best of us probably admits to some shortfall as they consider such a question.

As has been said, there may be all sorts of reasons for this. Lack of time, resources, support and the increased pressure and bureaucracy of the modern workplace are high amongst them. Enough. I will resist the temptation to indulge in an infinite list. Let us leave it that it is doubtless a complex picture, and of course one that varies over time and for every individual; doubtless affected also by local culture, where management practice can vary even in countries that exist as closely together as, say, Singapore and Malaysia.

Facing reality

Realistically no job, certainly no worthwhile job, one that is likely to appeal and provide job satisfaction, is strictly nine to five, enabling its occupant to go home each night with a clear in-tray and everything up to date.

In addition, in many jobs a significant amount of time will have to be spent dealing with, let us say, less than ideal circumstances. In other words, despite lack of resources or whatever, a way must be found and things made to happen so that targeted results are achieved. As my Mother used to say – *given oranges the job is to make marmalade.* Again you probably do this and do it well.

So be it. But, leaving that on one side for a moment, there is another reason why productivity and effectiveness is sometimes not maximised. The manager or executive – you – *allows* it to happen. Opportunities to get things done are missed and, worse, people often do not realise they are doing so. What is more, for reasons we have seen, today's job environment seems to be making this opportunity missing more likely. There is a process at work that, at worst, can produce a crisis in management effectiveness.

Before you protest that you are no part of the problem, consider. In Chinese writing, the word crisis is represented by two separate characters: in isolation the first means "chaos", and the second, interestingly, means "opportunity". An age old hint that if anything is wrong there is a possibility not only to remove the problem but to use the adjustment to improve things overall.

This book highlights an opportunity. It reviews a way of positively transforming and enhancing your performance virtually at a stroke. It focuses on approaches to those key things that should be done, and which are of a nature that will make overall success more likely. Here we examine some of the reasons why opportunities can be missed and highlight one approach that can change your practice in a way that affects many different situations positively. The aim is to allow you to recognise when performance can be improved, then be able to take action to free up potential and get more done and done well.

As the American philosopher William James said: *The greatest discovery of my generation is that a human being can alter his life by altering his attitude of mind.* Sometimes things get done only because they must be done (see below).

Interlude...

The following story makes a good point. An American college student is going on an exchange visit, swapping with a student from far away in a small town in northern Thailand. After much planning and preparation, and with some apprehension, she sets off on the long journey. After a long international flight, and a domestic flight, she is sitting in a car with her host travelling the final leg to the town where she will spend a year of her life.

She expresses her fears about the language, Thai being a notoriously difficult language to learn. Her host reassures her that she will manage it without difficulty, but, unconvinced, she is disbelieving. "It will surely not be difficult" he says "No-one in your host family speaks English. You have no choice; you *will* learn to speak Thai". The point here (also a very good insight into Thai culture) is that some things are best described not as difficult or easy, but simply as *necessary*. (See page 122 for the source of this story).

If it is essential, many things can be achieved.
Accepting that it is essential may be the first step.

Putting all this in context of the world of work in the twenty first century, and describing one approach that does just that, I have coined the phrase "managing in the discomfort zone" to describe taking purposeful action despite any awkwardness. So, if you are – for the moment – sitting comfortably …

$$\overline{\underline{2}}$$

Problems ... and opportunities

If you want to do something you find a way.
If you don't want to do anything, you find an excuse.

Arab proverb

To be a successful manager you need to work efficiently, productively, effectively and often creatively. Some of the things you do are, or have become, routine. While they must be done right, they can be done and done well without elaborate thought. You have other tasks, which may be one-off or regular, that are a challenge. They demand thought, and may demand struggle, but you are happy to view them this way. They all go on your work to do list and – sooner or later – they get done.

Between being accepted or listed to be done and actually being done may lie something of a muddle. Leaving aside the expertise you bring to bear, and how well you do things, the first foundation for success in terms of productivity – actually getting things done – is effective time management. This makes an appropriate starting point.

Managing your time

Time is a resource like any other; and an important one – respect for which can boost effectiveness and profitability. So, time management is a crucial skill. It can enhance productivity, allow you to focus on priorities and ultimately act directly to improve the effectiveness of individuals and the profitability of the firm. Making it work is dependent on a number of factors.

1. The inherent difficulties

So, if time management is so much common sense and so useful, why is not everyone a time management expert? Sadly the bad news is that the answer is that time management is difficult (but there is some balancing good news to come). The classic author G. K. Chesterton once wrote that the reason Christianity was declining was "not because it has been tried and found wanting, but because it has been found difficult and therefore not tried". Similarly with time management, there is no magic formula and circumstances – and interruptions – often seem to conspire to prevent best intentions from working out. Some people, perhaps failing to achieve what they want, despair and give up.

This is not an area in which you can allow perfection to be the enemy of the good. Few, if any of us, organise our time perfectly, but some are manifestly better at it than others. Why? Simply it is that those who are more successful have a different attitude to the process. They see it as something to work at. They recognise that the details matter. They consider the time implications of everything and they work to get *as close to their ideal of time arrangement as they can.*

Next week there can't be any crisis. My schedule is already full.

Henry Kissinger

16

Little things do mount up. Saving five minutes may not sound like much use, however do so every working day in the year (some 230 days) and you save nearly two and a half days! Speaking personally I could certainly utilise an extra couple of days, no problem. If time can be saved across a range of tasks, and for most people it can, then the overall gain may well be significant. The best basis for making this happen, and the good news factor I promised was to come, is that consideration of time and its management can be made a habit.

Now, habits are powerful. Ones than need changing may take some effort to shift, but once new ones are established, then they make the approaches they prompt at least semi-automatic. The process of getting to grips with managing your time effectively may well take a conscious effort, but by establishing good working habits it is one that gets easier as you go on.

2. The ubiquitous meeting

Perhaps nothing makes a better example of wasted time than that of business meetings, especially internal ones. Which of us cannot remember a meeting that we emerged from recently saying "What a waste of time!"? First there is the question of the time it takes most meetings to get underway. Scheduled for 2 – 00 pm people dribble in over the ensuing ten minutes, then a start is made, only to be interrupted five minutes later by a late arrival. There is a pause, a recap and the meeting begins again. We all know the feeling, I am sure. Yet, even having said that, I am conscious that attitudes differ to the overall question of punctuality per se: for example, when I conduct public courses in Asia the attitude of a group to late comers, and of the organiser, to just how long after the published start time one should begin, varies from the situation in the U.K. It remains a fact, however, that punctuality affects productivity directly.

Yet there is surely no reason for it to be like this. Some meetings can and do start on time. I can still remember an early boss of mine asking me join an important executive committee. Enthusiastically, I hastened to my first meeting, but could not find it. The scheduled conference room was locked and no one seemed to know where the meeting was being held. Meeting up with my boss later and explaining the problem, I remember he simply looked me straight in the eye and said, "When did you arrive?". The meeting was being held at the designated conference room – but he had locked the door! I was never late for one of his meetings again, and, barring real accidents, nor was anyone else. He not only believed it was important to start on time, he organised things accordingly.

> **Meetings are indispensable when you don't want to do anything.**
>
> *J. K. Galbraith*

This is a very good example of the effect of culture and habit within an organisation combining to save people significant time. For the record, meetings need:

- a starting time

- a finishing time (so people can plan what they can do afterwards and when)

- a clear agenda (maybe with timings for different topics and certainly circulated in advance)

- good chairmanship (to keep discussion on track)

- no distractions (to allow concentration – so organise refreshments beforehand and switch off telephones, especially mobiles).

And, above all, meetings need clear objectives. Ban any meeting with a time in its title – *"the monthly administration review meeting"* – they will just become a routine. Never have a meeting that is just *about* something. So you can convene a meeting to explore ways of increasing revenue by 5% in the last quarter of the year, but not one just to "increase profitability". With clear intentions, good time keeping and a firm hand on the tiller as it were, most meetings can be productive.

This attitude and approach can be taken in many areas. Respecting how things must be done if they are to be effective and organising so that the best way of working becomes a habit for all concerned is vital.

3. Plan the work and work the plan

The principles of good time management are not complex. Overall they can be summarised in three principles:

- List the tasks you have to perform

- Assign them priorities

- Do what the plan says.

It is the last, and to some extent the second also, that causes problems, so some other thoughts here may help. It may be useful to categorise tasks, putting everything that must be dealt with on the telephone, say, together. It is certainly useful to plan time for tasks as specifically as you schedule appointments. In conducting training on presentational skills I am regularly told by participants that there is never enough time to prepare. Yet this is a key task. Skimping the preparation, and making a lacklustre presentation can see weeks of time and work going down the drain. Putting the preparation time in the diary, setting aside a clear couple of hours or whatever it takes and sticking to that in a way that avoids interruptions must be worthwhile. Yes, this demands some discipline – more if it is a team presentation and colleagues must clear time to be together as they prepare – but it can be done, and it pays dividends. A similar principle applies in many different contexts.

The only way to be sure of catching a train is to miss the one before it.

G. K. Chesterton

It is a prime principle of time management that time must be invested to save time in the future. Sound preparation of a presentation may take two hours, but how long is involved in recovering from a "no" from the Board, or replacing a prospect if a client sales presentation goes wrong? No contest. And the same principle applies to systems; sorting something out so that it works well on a regular basis is also likely to be time well spent.

The last of the three main principles above is the one that needs most effort.

4. Staying "on plan"

There are two main influences that combine to keep you from completing planned tasks. They are other people and events, and you. Let us start with you. You may, for example, put off things because you:

- Are unsure what to do

- Dislike the task

- Prefer another task (despite the clear priority)

- Fear the consequences.

Or more, and time can be wasted in the reverse way. What tasks do you spend too long on (or resist delegating) because you *like* them? Be honest. Often this is a major cause of wasted time, as is flattering yourself that no one else can do something as well as you can (perhaps you do not delegate in case someone proves *more able* than you at it! It is a thought worth pondering). Such things may be one off or, worse in their potential for wasting time, regular. Certainly there are principles to be noted in this area: a main one is the fallacy that things get easier if left. Virtually always the reverse is true. Faced with sacking a member of staff to take a dramatic example, many people will constantly prevaricate. They may want to "see how things go", "check the end of month results" or some such, when swift action (all the checks in fact having been done) is best all round.

The second area of problems that keep you from key tasks involve the classic interruption. We all have some colleagues who, when they stick their heads round the door and say, "Have you got a minute?" mean half an hour minimum is about to vanish unconstructively. Saying no is an inherent part of good time management. Telephones can also be the bane of our lives (though think carefully about how voicemail in all its forms can dilute customer service at any stage of the relationship). But there are moments to be unavailable – some tasks can be completed in a quiet hour, yet take much longer if we are constantly interrupted. This applies especially to anything that requires some real thought or creativity, such as writing a report.

5. A major asset

Good time management is a real asset to anyone's productivity and effectiveness. It is worth exploring the possibilities, instilling the right habits and avoiding any dilution of your firm intentions. And results increase in an organisation where everyone is similarly motivated. The details, and there are many of them, are what make an overall sensitivity to managing time work well.

21

Space prohibits going further, but the rationale of time management underlies much of what follows here.

In limbo

The angst of struggling with something beyond its deadline is such a common feeling that it has even been given its own special name: ziargic tension. However, with some consideration, and having developed some good habits and work practices you will be productive and able to cope even with hectic situations. But few, if any, people are perfect at time management. A moment's muddle may be excused, but there are real exceptions, things that seem to avoid our best time management intentions altogether. What stays on the "to do" list longer? The list of things that remain to be done will contain some tasks that:

- timing rightly necessitates are not yet undertaken

- priorities dictate will be done shortly (even if not quite as soon as you would wish)

- are less important and must wait their turn (without problem)

- involve other people where their timing and circumstances influence when they are done and may act to delay matters (so that the preliminary of chasing others may become an item to progress in its own right).

You can probably think of more categories and extend the variety of the nature of reasons for delay that are involved – everything from waiting for someone to execute a necessary computer repair to the endless juggling necessary to arrange a meeting convenient to four people all with busy schedules, before you can move ahead.

22

An honest appraisal of what is on your "to do list" however will highlight another category; one where the key reason for delay is solely down to you. Why does this happen? One reason reoccurs.

Consider this fact:

Sensible, and logically necessary, action can be delayed or left untaken for no reason <u>other than that it seems difficult</u>.

We will define "difficult" further in a moment, meantime I know the response that saying such a thing instinctively prompts, so let us include it and allow the typical hardworking individual manager to have their say.

HARDWORKING MANAGER (HM): Wait a minute. Are you suggesting that I don't do things just because I find them difficult? I deal with difficult things all day; nothing about my job is easy I'll have you know, but I do it and I do it pretty well.

No one is suggesting management is easy, or that you are not striving to succeed. Quite the reverse, but the fact remains that there is often action that could be taken, that could make things better, and achieve results more certainly, and yet which is not done. Certainly it is not done in good time. Are you saying, for example, that there is nothing on your current "to do" list that you are a tad uncertain about or which you are putting off making decisions about? Or that there are not things where, while the action is clear, you know that taking it will make you, well, uncomfortable? For example, is none of your team under-performing in any way? Is nobody not following a rule or procedure, in a way that dilutes performance just a little?

HM: Well, yes, I suppose there are some things that do get put off, but life's more than a little hectic you know – surely that will always be the case? It doesn't mean I'm a bad manager.

No, indeed it does not, but there may be ways in which you can become a better manager, in which you can get more done, achieve better results and improve both how you feel about it and how others see you at the same time. But we are getting ahead of ourselves. I take your point; but let us consider first the situation in which you must work, after all anything you do must make sense and work in the real world.

And here the intention is to reflect the realities of the work place and identify key action, to an extent simple action, that can help you focus on the right things, and take action about them promptly in a way that will increase the likelihood of achieving the overall results you want.

HM: Okay, go on then. Certainly anything that helps is welcome.

The challenge of modern management

The challenging task that faces most people has already been addressed. You manage your job, and achieve what you do in the way you do for a number of reasons. Three areas are key here, all relate to your experience:

- **Knowledge.** What you know helps you act. For example, you make a good presentation in part because you know something of the tricks of the trade of so doing. You get your way at a meeting because of your knowledge about the way meetings work and what makes a message persuasive. You no doubt know a great deal, indeed it is easy to underestimate what you do know. Also specific knowledge underpins particular areas of your work. For example, hire someone and you need to know something about employment legislation or you may arrange things in an inappropriate way that lumbers you with a dud forever.

- **Skills.** Your expertise is, of course, based partly on knowledge, but more than that is involved. You need practice to do some things well; doing the job will make you better at it provided you approach it in the right spirit.

- **Attitude.** The attitude you take to things helps dictate effectiveness too. Some things need you to be persistent, self-motivated or thick skinned.

All these aspects of your competence combine, and are influenced by, the way you work. But that is not entirely an objective process. Human nature dictates otherwise. Who never allows positive personal feelings to influence how they work? Be honest. So in deciding to attend a conference in Singapore, to spend extra time on something they like, or to work most closely with those people they get on with best, it is possible that a manager is, in part at least, allowing what is best for them to be an element of the decision making. Sometimes this does no harm; it may even do good. Certainly it happens. So it is not so surprising that sometimes the reverse is true and decisions are made, not for positive personal reasons, but to avoid some negative effect.

Consider an example.

Example – the discomfort of wasting time

If something threatens to waste our time, we are more inclined to get impatient than truly uncomfortable. While this may be less dramatic than some other situations, It is, however, something that occurs all too often in a busy life – so, if change is desirable, the opportunity it presents may be considerable.

HM: I may not be perfect, but if there is one thing I am it's productive – no one gets through more in a day than I do.

And that may itself be a problem. Consider this. There is a scene that is played out in offices all over the world and which must waste untold hours every single day. Imagine a manager is busy in his office when a head comes round the door and one of their staff comes in. 'What is it?' they ask. And the reply is something like: 'I am not sure how to handle so and so and wondered if you would just check through it with me'. The manager thinks for a second. They are busy – in the middle of a job and not wanting to lose concentration – but they have already been interrupted. So their first thought is to minimise the interruption so that they can get back to work fast. It seems the easiest thing to do. So, if the matter allows, they spend a minute or two explaining what to do and then tell the other person to let them get on, and the brief impromptu meeting ends. This may be done kindly or abruptly, the effect is much the same, and the same manager may enact the scene many times in a day.

The rationale for this approach is personal: it is uncomfortable to have concentration disrupted and the action seeks primarily to minimise that discomfort.

But suppose the same manager is away from the office for a couple of days. In their absence people face similar situations. If their manager were in, they would go and ask. In their absence, they simply get on with the job. When the manager returns what do they find? A chain of disasters? A plethora of wrong decisions and misjudged actions? Very rarely. Rather things that would have been checked if they had been around have been actioned, and not only is no harm done, everything has probably gone perfectly well.

Think about it. I suspect this picture will ring bells with many, if not most, managers. Why does it happen? It is a classic case of thinking that it is quicker to do things for people: most often in this case providing an answer or making a decision. They then take action, and life goes on.

What this describes is essentially the taking of a short-term view. You have to take a longer-term view, but *doing so takes you instantly into what might be called the discomfort zone.*

Danger...

It is easy to think:

I must get my task finished (anything other than supplying an instant answer will take too long).

HM: Okay, I certainly get this sort of interruption and I guess that is how I think. But what else is there to do?

There is certainly another approach. It is one that looks beyond the short term and addresses longer-term and more important issues. It still saves time, though in the longer term, and achieves far more beyond this too.

HM: Go on.

Seven magic words

Next time you are interrupted in the way I have described, respond by saying something like: *'What do you think you should do?'*

The person who is interrupting may not know, but you can press the point, prompt them to make some suggestions, and when they do, then ask which solution they think is best. This takes a few minutes, certainly longer than a "leave me alone" response, but if they are coping when you are not there to ask, then you will find that when you prompt them they most often come up with a good answer (in business there is rarely any one right way). Then you can say something like: 'That's fine,' and away they go to carry on, leaving you to get back to your own work.

Now this is not just a better way of dealing with this situation. It brings additional results of very real value. It will:

- **teach people not to interrupt,** but rather to have the confidence to think matters through for themselves. You have to be insistent about this. It will not work if you only make them think it through when you have more time, and still provide a quick answer when you are busy. Every time – every single time – someone comes through the door with a question about something with which you believe they should be able to deal unaided, you say: 'What do you think you should do?' It must become a catch phrase. And as this practice continues the message will get home to them, so that if they even start to think of asking you they can hear your likely response in advance in their mind. If you do this you will find such questions coming less and less often. You will find that if people do ask, they move straight to the second stage, and come in with two or three thought out options just wanting you to say which is best. Resist; ask them. The message will stick and, surprise, surprise, you will find you are saving what may be significant time over the long term as the incidence of such interruptions declines.

- **teach them to analyse a situation and make decisions.** It will make people more efficient and more self-sufficient, and

28

this is good for overall productivity and the achievement of results (and for the people).

- **highlight any development areas that need addressing.** Thus if there is a real inability to take action because of some skill that is lacking, or inadequately developed, this can be addressed. This might be with a few words there and then, or need a longer session that can be scheduled soon. Alternatively the highlighting of any skills gap may lead to more fundamental action: for instance you need to organise for someone to undergo formal training, attending a course say.

I always pass on good advice. It is the only thing to do with it. It is never any use to oneself.

Oscar Wilde

- **have an ultimately positive motivational effect** too, because your people will almost certainly get to like taking more responsibility (and feeling able to do so), especially if you comment favourably on how well they are doing on the decisions that they are making unaided. This can add additional real benefit to the way action is taken.

This latter approach only needs some persistence and determination. But starting to work like this is unlikely to be entirely comfortable.

Danger...

And you may have to watch out for any other instinctive responses that put you off and rather aim to keep you comfortable by sticking with the simple "do this" approach:

- I'm not sure how to counsel in the right way

- The staff member will take it as criticism (and that will lead to an argument and take more time)

- I can't face any hassle at the moment.

Early on, if you begin to embrace such an approach, you may think such an approach is taking too much time, but the investment formula will surely pay off. There are considerable benefits to be had here, the number of people who report to you multiplies them. Do not be faint hearted about this, it is very easy to break your resolve in a busy moment and send someone on their way with an instant, dictated solution. Exceptions to your consistency will just make the lesson take longer to get over. But this idea really does work in the longer term; not to operate this way may seem to succeed in keeping you comfortable, but it does your people – and the results you can achieve together – a disservice. And all it takes is a resolve to move into the discomfort zone for sufficiently long to allow you to become comfortable about something new for the future.

Here, avoiding a moment's discomfort and taking a longer-term view can boost staff performance and morale (and save you time on an ongoing basis).

Interlude

The message unfolding is essentially a positive one. It focuses on positive action you can take to improve performance. The danger here is not simply procrastination – something we are all prone to occasionally. What exactly is procrastination?

A classic story serves to define it well:

A man is lying very ill in hospital. The doctors come and go, specialists are sent for, but no clue is discovered as to what the cause is of his illness. More tests are done, so many that his life becomes a routine: a test one day, the results a week later, then another test and another wait for the result. But there is still no cause discovered for his sickness. Then one Friday a doctor comes in and tells him, *"At last we know what's wrong with you. But I'm afraid we have some bad news – and also some very bad news – which do you want first?"* The man struggles to answer, *"Let's have the bad news,"* he says. *"Well, I'm afraid the test showed that you only have one week to live,"* says the doctor. *"My God,"* says the man, *"in that case, what on earth is the very bad news?"*

The doctor looks embarrassed: *"Well, we got the test result in last Thursday,"* he said. *"Err ... but ... we forgot to tell you."*

And that is certainly procrastination.

Here we focus on rather different reasons for action being delayed or skimped.

With one bound ...

What is being said here is straightforward. If things, especially things that are significant or key to results generation, are not done, performance will suffer. Perhaps major opportunities will be missed. A regular cause of things being not done (or at least not done when they should be done) is because we avoid them for fear that addressing them will be in some way uncomfortable.

Easy, you may say, let us just be sure this does not happen.

HM: Right, I understand what you are saying. I'll be careful.

In a hectic work life it is not that easy; or there would be no examples like the one above. To create improved performance by addressing this issue you need to understand:

- why this avoidance happens so easily

- what kinds of personal discomfort are most likely to be avoided

- how difficult, uncomfortable situations can be recognised

- what action to take to break the mould and ensure that action – the right action – is taken as and when it will do the most good

- how to identify and utilise opportunities and make them work for you.

The ensuing pages are designed to address these elements and provide a route to greater effectiveness.

Once upon a time

Once upon a time ...... there was a wolf. He was scruffy, bedraggled and generally down at heel. He scratched a living where he could, but was regarded by the other animals as very low in the pecking order. He hated this; he wanted to be well regarded and, after long fruitless hours trying to think how he could change his image, he concluded he needed some help. He asked an aardvark, an anteater and an antelope for advice. Nothing; though the antelope suggested that he asked the lion – after all he's the king of the jungle. Risky it might be, but he was desperate, so he went and – very carefully – approached the lion.

To be continued ...

3

Managers are human too

Chance favours the prepared mind.

Louis Pasteur

The first step to managing in the discomfort zone – taking decisive and appropriate action despite the feeling that doing so somehow puts us in an awkward, difficult or uncomfortable position – is to understand something of why this feeling occurs. This involves recognising that there is an inherent and, to a large extent, unconscious, process going on here. For the most part inaction or delay does not happen as part of an objective review: *let's leave that for the moment, I can't face it*. It happens for what is regarded at the time as "a good reason"; often no more is required than to decide that something else is more important. Maybe you will get to the thing eventually, but even slight delay may cause some problems and it is generally agreed that most difficult things do not get easier if left – rather they tend to become more (and more?) problematic.

It is said you should:

Never confuse activity with achievement.

Good advice. One danger here is that being busy, and always being able to find other things to do if something is sidelined, actually compounds the problem. It allows a rationalisation that says that any avoidance action is in fact "necessary".

If you are tempted to identify with this, even a little, do not despair – you are not alone. Indeed I would suggest that the fact that everyone does this is one of the reasons it remains a problem, or, let us be positive, that it remains an opportunity for potential improvement. Organisations are, in part, mutual support systems. Two heads are often better than one, not everyone has the same experience, and consultation and collaboration act like yeast in a loaf to get things working. But, while you may go to your manager and say *'can I have your opinion about this?'*, or even *'can you help with this?'*, you are much less likely to go and say *'I'm finding this really uncomfortable, will you get me out of it?'* Here we are reviewing an area that remains largely unaddressed by one of the most powerful and regular mechanisms that exists within organisations. Hence the necessity for everyone individually to address it in their own situation – and see what gain they can make, and what action is necessary to make them.

To make your task easier, consider what happens in your mind when you are faced with a typical discomfort situation.

Balancing needs

If sometimes we do not proceed logically, it is not because we are incapable of logic, rather because other factors submerge our logical thoughts, overpowering or cutting them off stillborn. This is a powerful – and natural – effect. It is one well recognised by psychologists and it should not be dismissed lightly. Recognising that it happens and that it needs dealing with in an active way is the first step to combating it, and thus to ensuring that a more considered path is followed.

What are the main triggers that prompt something to be put on one side? There are several:

- The overriding feeling is one of avoidance, the need to get away from the uncomfortable; see box. Not surprising really, who actually wants to be embarrassed, upset or otherwise put out? No one. We do not want to feel it and, even more, we do not want to be seen to feel it. So we see such situations coming and juggle with our lives to avoid them; albeit (if you like) subconsciously. It works too. Certainly in the short term, we do avoid the upset – but we avoid taking positive action about something too and that can cause a variety of problems.

"Uncomfortable"

The range of things we fear or avoid includes, in no particular order:

Embarrassment, confusion, criticism, confrontation (with someone aggressive, difficult or even simply that we are unsure of or do not know well), difficulty, distress, humiliation, uncertainty, frustration, ridicule, stress, doubt, perplexity, alarm – and being wrong, making a mistake, and all the consequences of that being seen and addressed by others. Add to taste.

All such feelings come in a variety of guises and a range of severities. Each of us may have worst fears, things we dislike disproportionately; and perhaps also some others we get over with little or no problem.

To escape criticism – do nothing, say nothing, be nothing.

Elbert Hubbard

36

- Another strong feeling is that of urgency. Modern life has created a short attention span. We live in a world of sound bites and instant hits and have come to reject the fact that some things cannot be instantly resolved. The result is that if something is not only likely to make us uncomfortable, but to take a moment to deal with too, then we are all the more likely to side track it, possibly in favour of something that can be sorted promptly; or several such somethings, which will give us a greater illusion of getting a lot done.

- The easy or straightforward tends to be allowed to displace the more difficult. This is true without what needs to be done being inherently uncomfortable. It occurs to me, writing this, that writing is a classic example of such displacement activity. Writers are notorious for putting off getting down to work. They do something difficult they reason, why not get a few easy things out of the way first. They sharpen their pencils (as a preliminary to working on a computer this has become a real nonsense!), they make more tea, they read (and call it research) – and it can all go on for a long time. But eventually the more difficult task must be started. The quotations (see box) make the point with regard to writing; though the second one works well if you substitute the word work for writing. If something is not just difficult, but truly likely to cause discomfort along the way, then the chances of likely avoidance is compounded.

I love deadlines, I love the whooshing noise they make as they go by.

Douglas Adams (author of The Hitchhiker's Guide to the Galaxy), famous for putting off writing.

37

> **I write when I'm inspired, and I see to it that I am inspired at nine o'clock every day.**
>
> *Peter De Vries*

- The other main cause of delaying or skimping tasks is lack of knowledge or skill – not knowing quite how to proceed. This sparks fear, fear felt internally and externally – I might get this wrong and what will people think? Most people, in most jobs, have to tackle new things. It can be difficult, but the rewards are likely to be good. Once you can do something then being able to do so, and do so well, may open up possibilities that are both job and career enhancing. Nevertheless the initial worry is very real and is certainly instrumental in seeing things put off to their detriment. Incidentally, it is not a question of black and white. You may have some skill but it is inadequate to doing a comfortable, fear free, job. For example, I conduct many training courses on presentation skills. Most participants know something about it, but they want greater skill to allow it to be done quickly and easily – and allow them to excel. Equally, the additional knowledge or skill improvement required to allow positive action may be minimal and easily acquired, but the fact that that stage exists means that the chances of delay increase.

A further thing to watch out for, one of surprising power, is using things that you like to keep you away from others. Many people have the tendency to spend more time than is strictly necessary on tasks that they enjoy (and also to resist delegating things that could be passed on for the same reason) – if you doubt this ask yourself might you just regard attending a conference that involves a long grisly motorway journey differently from one that takes you somewhere exotic: Singapore, London or New York, say? Sometimes people go further and use this to camouflage and sideline jobs that are more demanding of attention, but which are less appealing or a positively uncomfortable prospect.

Mentioning fear leads us to another important and separate issue: that of stress.

The stressful workplace

Most management jobs are no picnic. There is a great deal to do and plenty of obstacles to contend with along the way. In recent years the pressure seems, as discussed in the Introduction, to have increased. So be it. No really interesting and rewarding job is cushy and strictly nine to five (though do let me know if you know of one!). Life and work are hectic and may be none the worse for that – succeeding despite this is one cause of satisfaction.

Sometimes, however, the pressure becomes less than easy to cope with. The job may inherently generate stress, but it does not follow that you have to spend your life feeling stressed out. What matters is your reaction to pressure. There has become a worrying acceptance in many a workplace that stress, meaning unwarranted stress, is a given – something that simply goes with the territory. This is, in my view, wholly the wrong view to take.

Things are going to get a lot worse, before they get worse.

Lily Tomlin

An unwarranted – disruptive – level of stress is undesirable. It actively reduces productivity and efficiency, and it lowers motivation and probably staff retention too. It needs to be worked against and everyone involved shares a responsibility for doing so.

Leaving that on one side for the moment, consider the negative cycle of stress in the work place in the context of our theme. People, not surprisingly, react personally; they are concerned with their own well-being. So, they:

- **avoid things that will increase their stress levels.** This directly relates to putting off difficult issues; not only are they seen as individually difficult (embarrassing or whatever), they are also seen as certain causes of a heightened stress level. Procrastination flows in a way that seems all too logical.

- **indulge in ritual,** that is in a myriad of behavioural patterns that are the equivalent of the writer sharpening their pencils. Some of these are personal, others are endemic in organisations where someone suggesting unnecessarily – *'let's organise a meeting (a committee or a study) first'* – is both accepted as normal, if not sensible, and is almost guaranteed to formalise prevarication. Perhaps there should be a phrase coined: **institutional prevarication**; perhaps it exists, maybe we should form a committee to check it out. Enough; sorry, I digress.

- **act the ostrich.** People may ignore things that need to be done but will be stressful, they do not even rationalise it or think of a good reason for delay. They forget it and hope it will go away, or somehow be easier when it does surface and demand attention (and are usually wrong on both counts).

- **give up or crack up.** The stress gets to some people so much that they retreat in some way: they become a poor attender, with health problems that are imagined or real. They become disruptive (blaming others is typical) or the gin and tonic they think will dilute the stress becomes a drink problem.

Not everyone goes down anything like this path, of course, but some do and perhaps many could. Addressing the issues in the right way and at an early stage is the best way to avoid any danger of being inadvertently nudged onto the dark path.

I do not intend to divert into a full thesis on managing stress (in any case I am no expert, preferring to concentrate on not allowing it to happen; I do not conduct any of the many "stress management" seminars that seem to abound these days, my belief that the best solution is not to worry about it being likely to create a somewhat brief event). Suffice to say that, in the context of the present message it should be recognised that:

Over stressful reactions to difficult work situations simply exaggerate the problems and cause a spiral of negativity.

Forewarned is forearmed

So, after all this what should we conclude? This kind of prevarication is axiomatic. It will happen and needs dealing with. Even one task dealt with positively and promptly rather than not, can improve performance significantly. The antidote is awareness of the problem and a logical approach. This raises, in turn, the question of how to ensure you take a logical view.

A considered approach

Without a doubt those who make the best managers, and by that I mean work most effectively, take a logical view of the task. Of course emotions are involved, of course creativity is necessary, and is a difficult concept to tie down (though there are logical approaches to ensuring ideas are generated), but many things need to be well considered, well balanced and well related to the reality of the situation.

41

There is room for the hunch, certainly for the hunch to play a part, though even a hunch may spring, in part at least, from the instinctive logic of proven habit. But a systematic and realistic approach is at the heart of many management processes. The checklist encapsulating good decision-making shown in the box makes a good example, and is also chosen as a topic worth a moment's thought in context of our main theme.

Decision-making

Decision-making is important in the context of this book in two separate ways. First, the quality of the decisions you make in your job will directly affect your effectiveness and success and, in turn, your career. Secondly, how decisions are made is a good example of logic working to make management work well.

To a degree there are no "right" answers in business, but there are certainly wrong ones. Experience is a vital factor in guiding us to pick the right alternative, though too much reliance on it can give a false sense of security and may stifle creativity. A procedure that is logical and systematic and that ensures due consideration of the alternatives, whilst not being infallible, will certainly help make more of your decisions turn out right. This leads to what is a neatly ten-step approach:

Step 1 Setting objectives

Before any action can be considered, the objectives of the exercise must be set. Unless you know where you are going, you cannot plan how to get there or how to measure your progress. For the objective to be valuable, it must be as specific and as quantitative as possible. Goals such as "increasing sales", "improving customer service" or "reducing costs" are useless, as they provide no basis for measurement.

42

If the aim is to increase sales, it should be specified by how much and within what time period.

Step 2   Evaluating the objective against other company objectives

When a clear, precise goal has been established, it should be compared with other organisational aims to ensure compatibility. Failure to do this is common, particularly in large organisations. This results in different sections of the firm working towards objectives which in themselves are reasonable, but which when put together become mutually exclusive: for example, the sales office manager may be trying to maintain business with small accounts, whereas marketing or sales management are planning to service them exclusively via wholesalers.

Step 3   Collecting information

Information can now be collected from which plans can be developed. It is unwise to start this data collection stage until clear, compatible objectives have been defined, otherwise vast quantities of useless figures will be assembled "for information" or "in case we need them". The hunger for information has been stimulated by various factors, including the advance of research techniques and the progressive development of the computer. It is a great temptation to the manager to call for information simply because he knows it is available. Mountains of figures may give a sense of security, but information is costly to process and is only useful (and economic) when it contains answers to precise questions, which have direct bearing on the decisions it is possible to take.

Step 4   Analysing the information

It is the objective that will guide the manager towards the questions to be answered and thus the information needed. The lines of analysis to be followed will in turn be indicated by such questions. For example, declining sales in one area of the country, perhaps owing to the larger customers buying from competitors, should not prompt us to ask for "everything we know about the market". What we really need is sales in that region broken down by customer type, possibly compared with similar figures for another area. From this analysis, we can proceed progressively through the relevant information, very much more precisely (and probably more quickly and economically) than starting with a dozen different breakdowns that attempt to show "all about everything".

Step 5   Developing alternatives

The whole basis of this method of approach is to encourage the manager to think more broadly and creatively about possible solutions to problems. Sometimes, of course, the solution will become obvious from systematic processing of the data. In the majority of instances, however, no clear-cut answers will be found, a number of factors suggest themselves, or the answer lies in a combination of a number of factors.

Step 6 Choosing the "best" alternative

This is the heart of the decision-making process. It is unlikely that all possible solutions can be implemented; one must be chosen. To help in this choice, consideration should be made of four criteria: Cost, time, risk and resources. The costs of each alternative can be calculated and compared against the objective.

Assuming that several approaches appear to be capable of achieving the objective, this might only narrow the choice. So the other yardsticks should also be used. Time taken might be a critical factor, or the element of risk (particularly of failure) or lack of certain resources might rule out other options: for example, a critical staff situation in an office may preclude certain courses of action.

The choice of the "best" alternative then is based on a consideration of all the advantages and disadvantages of all the possible alternatives. It is at this stage that experience can be particularly valuable. Its possible limiting effect will already have been overcome by the systematic search for alternatives.

Having made the choice, at least the manager will be well aware of what they have done in terms of the possible drawbacks of their decision and the discarded alternatives. It will also be easier at some time in the future, to look back and assess why such a decision was, in fact, made.

Step 7 Communicating the decision

This is a step too often omitted. And yet unless all concerned know what is being done, impact will be lost. For example, it is commonplace to find inside sales staff whose first knowledge of an advertising campaign is gained from customers; other such situations abound around organisations. The communication must be systematically planned. Information may well have to be passed by different methods and in different forms to different people, in writing, by telephone, meetings, etc. By communicating only necessary information by the most appropriate methods, far better results will be gained than by a blanket memorandum with copies emailed to everybody.

Step 8 Setting up the control system

Remember that this stage occurs before implementation. This is because in many cases the process of implementing a plan destroys the ability to evaluate it. For example, in a situation where it is believed that, say, inside sales staff lacks product knowledge, the decision might be taken to run a training programme. At the end of the course a test is given in which the average score is 90 per cent. It might be concluded, therefore, that the programme was successful. But, as there has been no measurement of what the test score would have been at the beginning of the programme, it can at this stage never then be known whether it was successful or not.

Step 9 Implementing the decision

Putting the decision into action should now be easy. It will have been clearly stated what is to be done towards what objective and why that particular action has been chosen, all concerned will have been informed, and the system of evaluation will have been set. Research has shown that if change is to be implemented, then specific tasks should be allocated to particular people and deadlines laid down for the tasks to be completed. Vague requests for action "sometimes", will inevitably result in failure.

Step 10 Evaluating the decision

Again assuming quantitative objectives, clear decisions and predefined control systems, evaluation is simple. The problems of control and evaluation in management are caused by lack of clear yardsticks against which to compare. If the manager simply sets broad qualitative goals of increasing sales "as much as possible" or improving customer service, they will have the utmost difficulty in evaluating the results.

There will usually be no common definition of what constitutes an increase or an improvement.

You need to make the "right" decision more often than not, and you may also benefit from a reputation for being decisive. So, never say Leave it with me and then fail to revert back. Rather, give things due consideration and make your consideration systematic, thorough – and logical.

Note: it is sometimes said of certain managers that they are too inclined to "play it safe", whether this is true or not it is worth noting that sometimes an element of risk exists; it is simply not possible for careful decision making to remove it. Accept it and act despite it.

Logical thought is useful and may need either to be cultivated or to be focused upon in a way that screens out some of the distractions already mentioned.

Contrariwise ...if it was so, it might be; and if it were so, it would be: but as it isn't, it ain't. That's logic.

Tweedledee in Lewis Carroll's Alice through the Looking-Glass

What allows the ability to think logically? Certainly the following are key:

- **A high tolerance to the realities of life.** Frustration is likely the order of the day in most jobs. Things never go the way you expect and, to quote Murphy's law, – *if something can go wrong it will* (see box for the full version). That said –

what are you going to do about it? Constantly resenting reality and hoping it will not be as it is fruitless. It really helps to develop a streak of realism. Recognise the facts of the matter as a starting point and it becomes much easier to take a logical view. Incidentally, watch out if you have perfectionist tendencies. These can be irreplaceable in attending to detail, but can compound frustration when, realistically, nothing will ever be exactly as you want. Constitutional perfectionists need to work hard to define perfection as something specific. Setting a measurable and considered level of quality say, the achievement of which allows satisfaction, rather than aiming for an ever receding goal that is never achieved but which can consume endless time as it is pursued.

Despair is the price one pays for setting oneself an impossible aim.

Graham Green

Murphy's Laws

These, their origins lost in the mists of time, appear in many forms. This version makes them number a neat ten.

1   If anything can go wrong, it will do so.

2   Nothing is ever as simple as it seems.

3   If you mess with something for long enough, it will break.

4   If you try to please everybody, somebody won't like it.

---

5 Nothing ever works out exactly as you expect.

6 Whatever you want to do, there is always something else you have to do first.

7 If you explain something so that no one could possibly misunderstand, someone will.

8 Nothing is certain until it has happened (and then you should check it more than once).

9 If everything is going according to plan, then it is a sure sign that something is about to go wrong.

10 The only predictable thing about your day is that something totally unexpected will happen.

- **Self belief.** Confidence in your abilities is a great facilitator of the ability to stand back, see the broad picture and address the situation logically. Confidence may need to be cultivated, but nothing succeeds like success; if you are doing well and achieving your goals, then it is easier to have confidence to continue and do more. Confidence can be instilled as a habit, though realistically it may need action to maintain and enhance it from time to time. Incidentally, nothing boosts confidence more than practical measures: acquiring the right knowledge, knowing you have an appropriate skill or that you are well prepared, for instance.

- **Acceptance of uncertainty.** To a degree this is closely linked to the first point. Wherever we may be we live in a dynamic world, and certainly in the workplace the vagaries of everything, from markets and competition to a clash of internal objectives between different departments in the same organisation, means dealing with the unexpected just goes

49

with the territory. Again acceptance and realism in the face of this fact helps you focus on logical responses. Thrashing about and retaliating, kicking against what may seem like "unfair" happenings hardly makes considered action likely.

- **Willingness to take risks.** Just as the unexpected should be expected, so nothing you initiate is guaranteed to succeed. If you wait on many issues for guarantees, you wait forever. Sometimes – regularly? – you have to take a chance. But the chances of success are much greater when in doing so you base action on sound experience and considered judgement. Again logical thinking provides an antidote to the mess of reality.

If the creator had a purpose in equipping us with a neck, he surely meant us to stick it out.

Arthur Koestler

- **Acceptance of change.** Everyone is in favour of change, you are surely no Luddite and want to work in an environment that changes and develops rather than one that is static and boring. Change is good. But go into someone else's office and say: We are going to have to make some changes here, and see what reaction you get! Ten to one it is defensive. Fighting against change instead of working with it is never going to help you take a logical view, especially if the fight is irrational or essentially emotional – I don't like it! (Or, more likely, you assume you don't like it)

- **Balancing the long and short term.** Many things seem to evoke a response in managers that is primarily short term.

Yet not only does a logical view surely demand assessing the two alongside each other, it is likely that a solely short-term view (which can be the instinctive response) may be inappropriate or damaging. The process of writing this book makes a good illustration. Any writing job has an element of the chore about it, yet if the opportunity to do so was rejected simply on this ground, then much could be missed longer term. Think of the royalties rolling in over the years (I wish!), and the other advantages (for me, writing fits very well alongside training work, and other things give other advantages, for example an overseas edition of a book may enhance my image in a location which, while I visit it regularly, is not my base).

The net effect of coming to terms with all these factors, is that you will be much more on top of the way you have to work; and conversely less stressed. Consider how often the stress of a particular situation is compounded by the fact that you are resentful and wishing something could be otherwise, aiming perhaps at an impossible ideal, when:

The ultimate antidote to stress is addressing the reality of a situation and basing practical action on the actual position that exists; and then being content that you have done just that and not worrying about it.

So far so good: view things in the right light and there is far less tendency to put off key tasks, avoid problems or generally neglect anything important. But there is another problem.

Office politics

People mean politics. If the office with no office politics exists, it has not been discovered yet, so the only option for those working in an organisation is to recognise this and act accordingly. No one can ignore any of the realities of life and survive for long, much less prosper, and the existence of office politics is certainly a reality.

Office politics has predominantly negative connotations (though not exclusively as we will see). The phrase itself summons up images of back stabbing, of Machiavellian plotting and watching your back.

What has been said about managers and executives being judged by results puts this in context. To be successful, to achieve the results you intend or hit the targets you are set, may well be a constant challenge. Certainly in increasingly competitive markets and unpredictable economic conditions this seems likely for many, if not most, people. The phrase *"the only place where success comes before work is in the dictionary"* is usually attributed to the hairdresser Vidal Sassoon; whoever said it first, it is usually true for most of us. Yet whatever work – hard work – is necessary in management, and whatever skills must be cultivated to back up pure application, the challenge remains – and if circumstances and people conspire to make the task more difficult, this cannot be ignored.

Now, let us be clear. There is nothing wrong with healthy competition between people in most cultures. Many would claim competition is good, and certainly it is another simple fact of human nature. Nor is friction necessarily all bad. It can act as a catalyst to stimulate consideration and creativity; it can prompt ideas and make things happen that might otherwise not. While the worst aspects of office politics are certainly unconstructive, in some ways it can work for you. But in either case these are not effects that should be regarded as "just happening". An active

52

approach is necessary to minimise the negative effects that office politics may have on you, and to maximise any constructive ways in which it may help you.

A politician is an animal that can sit on a fence and keep two ears to the ground.

H. L. Menkin

Let us examine for a moment how such constructive individual action should be approached. It is certainly not intended here to set out a "backstabbers' charter", rather to offer guidance to those wanting to increase their effectiveness and maximise any opportunities or methods able to assist overcome difficulties or promote success, and ultimately to help you to survive and thrive in your career. Several things are important:

1. Mixed intentions

People, however constructively they approach their jobs, are not motivated solely by the desire to meet objectives and succeed in achieving the results they are charged with producing. They have their own agendas. Some of these intentions will help the general good, but others may not. Such intentions include a wide range of factors.

Personal ambitions include:

- getting the job done

- increasing personal job satisfaction

- organising greater visibility

- impressing others

53

- securing greater rewards

- gaining greater authority

- taking on greater responsibilities

- beating others in a race for promotion

- obtaining additional perks.

The list above immediately shows the possibilities. A number of the points listed clearly involve the possibility of competition. One person gets more responsibility, takes on the authority to handle something or is selected to attend the important conference being held in Hong Kong – whatever; and another does not. Of course, all such matters are highly personal. One person might regard travel to a certain location as a perk, while another might see it only as a chore. Both might see personal advantage in being present at the meeting that takes place there.

As such outcomes are sought, people work hard to achieve what they want and it is a short step from simply pushing for it to pushing harder – not just in a way that achieves what they want, but in a way that prevents or handicaps someone else achieving their intentions. Assertiveness becomes aggression, and brute force then sometimes becomes the order of the day. What is done may be secretively devised, subtly and maybe even invisibly deployed, but brute force still describes it well – it has no purpose other than to achieve parochial personal advantage.

In addition, other factors may be at work also. Some people are inherently less concerned about others than they might be, some are made so by their own feelings of inadequacy or incompetence (real or imagined), and some may have what is frankly best described as a destructive streak.

2. People may be destructive

People may have all sorts of feelings, they may:

- want others to fail

- delight in others' misfortunes

- see winning as necessitating someone else losing

- use others

- like the process of "doing someone down" (regardless of any positive benefit to them)

- be bullies

- want the credit for everything

- let their prejudices overrule practicality

Again the nature and scale of all this may vary. Someone may simply be a bit ruthless in the way they set out to achieve some small step (like gaining the ubiquitous key to the Executive washroom). Or, at worst, they may see an out and out back stabbing approach as their best route to promotion, say, and be prepared to go to any lengths to succeed.

3. Appearances can be deceptive

Because of the way people approach their jobs, and because of many peoples' willingness to indulge, at least to some extent, in a political approach to what they do, it pays to remember that many of the signs around you in the organisation may be deceptive. Things are just not always what they appear, and what is said may contain hidden messages and hidden agendas.

We all know the stock warnings. Always be wary of the person who starts by saying *"Trust me"*, *"Let me be honest"* or

"I'm on your side"; or at least react with a clear intention to read carefully between the lines as the communication continues. Aim to understand peoples' motives, and do not necessarily automatically think the best of them, or give them the benefit of the doubt. Prudence is a good watchword in the political jungle of the typical organisation.

So, one element of your judgement about everything needs to be to keep an eye on the political implications or possibilities. This might be best stated as watching for dangers and opportunities, because what you observe may provide an indication of either. People need to be regarded as potential friends, or enemies; and sometimes they may be one on one occasion and another at a later time.

4. You need to watch the signs

You should aim to watch for, and read, any signs that may prove useful indicators, for example noticing:

- what is said

- how it is said

- announcements and decisions

- alliances and changes of alliance

- people's intentions and motivations

- the behaviour of others

- communications (from memos to meetings)

What you must do is link your own clear intention, purpose and objectives to a way of working that reflects the environment – that is the political environment. You cannot work in isolation in the sense of pursuing your intentions as if others cannot affect your progress towards them. They will. Assume they will. The only question is whether others can assist your progress or, alternatively, whether you need to prevent it being made less likely by others. Then, in either case, you need to consider what action might be necessary on your part to accentuate the positive.

In all sorts of ways this view needs to colour your judgement. For example, who – exactly – do you take into your confidence, and how much and how soon? When should you ask advice and from whom? How much should you publicise your success (or hide anything that is less than successful)? Who should you know and who should know you? And what do you want other people to think of you? All these sorts of question, and more, are important. All demand you make considered judgements. And that, in turn, demands you have your ear to the ground and know what is going on – or, better still, know what is about to go on.

5. Adopting an appropriate approach

The out and out obvious politician may be adopting an approach that does them more harm than good. Most organisations contain some individuals who are well known for their ruthless opportunism and politicking. Other people may sensibly avoid them, or at least avoid crossing swords with them or running foul of them. Their ploys are largely anticipated and ultimately may do them no good.

You have to decide just how to play things. Adopt the brash approach illustrated above and you may gain nothing. Avoid or ignore all the intrigue and you may be left on the sidelines and others will get the better of you. Just what is the best way forward? The specific approach you adopt will depend to some extent on the style of those around you, and the culture of the organisation you work in. Openness, for example, could be an advantage in a normally secretive environment, but might upset someone who was unable to envisage anything other than a secretive approach.

Certainly your approach needs to consider others. This does not include only prime players. It includes some others who, while themselves more neutral in the overall game plan, are potentially a source of help in specific ways. People add to your knowledge and competence in all sorts of ways; you need to actively cultivate a useful network of advisors, collaborators and people able to assist in any way.

Take the people out of an organisation and nothing of significance would be left. A network of people is the foundation resource of your corporate survival strategy. Having the right network cannot be left to chance. You need to have clear intentions, make and maintain the necessary contacts, use them systematically and keep some records to help facilitate the whole process. If this makes it seem somewhat scheming; then so be it. It is necessary. But it is also an important part of organisational life.

People, and your contacts and interactions with particular ones, are what makes working in an organisation possible, interesting and fun. But:

The politics that inherently goes with organisational working abounds with areas that create discomfort.

Worrying about who is on your side, who will object, seek to score points and make life uncomfortable in many, many ways – right up to wanting your job – all provide reasons to avoid the discomfort. There is a wide range of rewards stemming from being realistic about office politics and taking an active approach to appreciate how it works and deal with it.

Certainly there are many discomfort factors stemming from the overall political environment, and a high chance that they are the kind that are apt to be dismissed as unreal. We do not actually take on board that we are avoiding getting involved with or doing something simply because, for example, we fear confrontation with a certain individual. Realism about the entire fabric of the situation in which you work needs to be born in mind if you are to be truly effective.

The way forward

Overall you have to find a way of working that enables you to compensate for matters of human nature where instinct tends to promote inappropriate thinking or action. You need to operate effectively across all the things you have to do, and avoid anything that encourages you to isolate and file some things away in a "for action when things are better" place. The right frame of mind is essential. Given the instinctive tendencies to go in the other direction, some positive thoughts about the way ahead may be appropriate to end this chapter. So:

- **Focus on the good results.** Note what works and what you make go well, link the past with the future – this is like so and so, that worked out okay, so let's make this do the same. This habit of comparison can become an important and useful element of your logical approach.

- **Set clear priorities.** It is a fact that, while several (many?) projects can be edged along in parallel, at any one moment you can only do one thing at a time. Choosing which must be done when in light of the relative priorities of everything you have on the go is vital. Such decisions must, in turn, reflect clear overall job objectives. If you are unclear about any aspect of those, then you must – repeat must – seek to clarify your brief. The alternative is for anything you try to do to be either considered in isolation and suffer from it, or at loggerheads with the doubtless long total list of things to be done. That way lies confusion and failure. The principle of having clear objectives and a clear brief apply equally to individual projects. As a useful aside see the boxed note about what makes for clear objectives below.

Objective setting

The oldest management maxim of all says that if you do not know where you are going any road will do. Setting clear and appropriate objectives is a key part of planning almost anything; something that literally creates a foundation for success. A much-quoted acronym can provide a good guide here: SMART. This stands for:

> **S**pecific
> **M**easurable
> **A**chievable
> **R**ealistic, and
> **T**imed.

As an example you might regard objectives linked to your reading of this book as:

- To enable you to spot danger areas where potential discomfort may delay action and deal with such situations positively *(specific)*

- To ensure *(measurable)* action takes place afterwards (here you might link to any appropriate measure: from agreements or actions that follow dealing with something to the actual results, perhaps described by figures or finances, that accrue)

- To be right for you: sufficient, understandable, information in manageable form that really allows you to change and improve what you do later (an *achievable* result)

- To also be *realistic*, that is desirable – hence here a short book of short sections, (if it took you several days to read the effort might prove greater than any benefit coming from doing so)

- And *timed*; always a good factor to include in any objective – by when are you going to finish reading this book? When can you address something differently as a result? How far ahead of doing so should you prepare?

So, ask yourself whether you are clear in this respect before you even begin work on a task. If you know why something must be done, and what you intend to achieve then you are well on the way to success. Time spent sorting this, and making sure you have a clear vision of what the objectives are, is time well spent. It may only take a few moments. Or it may need more thought and take more time. So be it. It is still worth doing and in any case may well save time at a later stage. Certainly setting inadequate objectives, and then discovering half way through that you are unsure quite where you are going and then having to take time to rethink is unlikely to be a productive way of working.

- **Manage your key resource** – time – effectively. The approaches and systems of time management are key to success for any busy manager (there was some detail about this in the last chapter; and it will be referred to again in the next, because effective time management itself can be a difficult, sometimes uncomfortable, process).

- **Give yourself some rewards.** The principle of self-motivation is a valid one. The reward can be great or small. For example, I have promised myself a nice cup of tea and a biscuit when I have completed the draft of this chapter and it is surprising how even something as simple as that concentrates the mind (provided it is a chocolate biscuit, of course!). My compulsion for chocolate apart (I've always regarded chocolate as compulsory), this perhaps makes a good example. This can be used actively as you first identify areas of avoidance, and then focus on making sure that you grasp the discomfort nettle, as it well, and take appropriate action.

- **Organise to maximise job satisfaction.** The more you enjoy your job, the more you will tend to be on top of it. Things are less likely to slip between the cracks if you are well-organised and up to date on things. There is an old saying that, it is difficult to see the writing on the wall, when your back's to it. The antithesis of this is that if you are on top of things, you are better placed to take things forward together, prevent anything being misplaced along the way, and ensure that things are well done; indeed that everything is well done. The same applies, of course, to the effectiveness of any team of people you may manage: your making their jobs' satisfying – motivating them well – is an important part of your job and one well worth the time it takes.

I have not meant to harp exclusively on the difficulties in this chapter. It is surely part of a logical approach to management to be realistic: realistic about the workplace and realistic about yourself. There are tendencies, which – for us all – make sidelining difficult issues, sometimes even those that are essentially simple tasks, seem like the natural thing to do. It is human nature to seek to minimise difficulty – to avoid the discomfort trap. And, let us be honest, some of what makes for discomfort in management makes for considerable discomfort. Positively, if we recognise this and work at overcoming these tendencies, then we are well on the way to ensuring that everything we do gets due attention – and works – not just those things that are routine, straightforward or fun.

Pressure is only pressure if you cannot control it.

John Parrott

Now first, as I said earlier, for me it is a cup of tea and a biscuit; then the next chapter reviews more about the type of task where opportunity for improved performance exists if initial discomfort is addressed.

Once upon a time (continued)

The mangy wolf sidled obeisantly up to the lion, determined to get an answer. Err, excuse me, sorry to interrupt Your Majesty, but I need your help. I want people to like me, I don't want to be thought of as just a miserable, scruffy lowlife; I want to be loved. What can I do? Please advise me, your Majesty, please, he said. The lion was clearly irritated by the interruption. He looked annoyed. For a moment he consider violence. Then …

To be continued …

4

Issues to address

There is always a well-known solution to every human problem – neat, plausible ... and wrong.

H. L. Menkin

Where can you put the philosophy of managing in the discomfort zone and dealing with difficult things to work? Where in fact can you aim to get uncomfortable and benefit from it? You are searching for areas within your work portfolio that are, for one reason or another, likely to be sidelined or neglected just because *they might make you uncomfortable.* Such areas need not be significant for it be worthwhile you taking a new view of them (after all we are not talking about a great expenditure of time, cost or effort), though the results will be most dramatic with matters that are important. Better still if, in turn, they are things that link directly to your ability to create the results that you want.

Some such areas will be particular to your own job, but here I will comment on ten generic and intentionally disparate examples, chosen as likely to be of importance to many readers, and all of which lend themselves very much to the principles described here. Indeed they are chosen, in part, to demonstrate a range of different degrees and types of discomfort. Let us start with something important to many people: networking (all of us are assisted by a good network of contacts and this needs originating and sustaining).

Ten kinds of issue to address

1. Networking

There is an old saying that "it is not what you know, but who you know that counts". In the world of work this certainly contains an element of truth. The term networking encompasses the whole process of getting in touch with people and maintaining and developing that contact to the mutual benefit of both parties. Let us take one element of that: an external one. Consider the following example.

Imagine that you are scheduled to attend a management conference of some sort. It may focus on a topic that is important to you and which interests you. You look forward to hearing what is said and have in mind uses for the information you will gather.

In addition, like so many people in such a position, you hope you may meet people there who are themselves of interest to you or valuable in some way (maybe they are potential customers or collaborators; maybe you hope to meet your next employer). You do not just hope to meet such people – you intend to do so. So, off you go, ready to do just that.

What happens? The next day you sit down back at your desk surrounded by all the bumph from the conference, and one solitary business card. This is from the person who happened to be sitting next to you, with whom you exchanged a few words at the mid-morning coffee break, and who was of no possible future interest whatsoever.

Why was this? Was it just the luck of the draw, with two hundred people there was it just unlucky that you did not sit next to someone more useful? Or does the reason lie elsewhere?

Almost certainly it is the latter. Why did you not return with ten business cards, or twenty? The personal discomfort factor here is a common one: embarrassment. If you are at all typical you looked round you and rationalised the opportunity away: *they don't look as if they would be helpful – I'm sure they would snub me – That person looks rather unapproachable – I'm not sure what to say – I can't interrupt the conversation those two are having.* This attitude can vary in degree. For some people it is worse in a social or semi-social situation – like a cocktail party or refreshment time ahead of a business breakfast meeting.

Yet is making what happens different really so difficult? All it needs is a little resolve. So:

- Resolve to network actively

- Be clear about the kind of person with whom you want to establish contact

- Set yourself a target (ten new contacts from today's conference or whatever)

- Plan some introductory remarks (questions may be best – from where they are from to what they thought of a particular session – but make them open ones, that is questions that cannot be answered by "yes" or "no" and are thus more likely to prompt a dialogue)

- Consider what can make your contact memorable and always follow up and keep in touch over time if you do not want contacts to wither and die

- Monitor results so that you have past successes in mind when you approach someone new.

Thinking through what is necessary – a systematic approach that will make what needs to be done a little easier and certainly more effective – is worthwhile. Some people develop particular methods, approaches that become habits, to help maximise their effectiveness. For example, someone I regard as an excellent networker always carries a pocket voice recorder. If he meets someone at an event, he gets their card, then as he moves on he dictates a sentence or two as a reminder and then makes some notes about how the contact might be valuable when he gets back at his office. He is never left, as so many of us are, wondering – *who was it who said that ... was he the one with the moustache or the funny spectacles?*

This is a very typical "discomfort area" and improvement here can be useful to many people; even one more contact could prove useful. Like many areas touched on here, this is something about which further study may well be useful; for the record, in my opinion the best book on networking is *Brilliant Business Connections* (Frances Kay, How to Books).

Embarrassment can also prevent action in other areas, similar in nature, such as cold calling and making follow up contact designed to prompt action or commitment from people with whom you are already in touch (though such may demand more specific persuasive or sales skills as well as simply a positive commitment to take action). Following up existing contacts is an allied area that can present difficulty and allows me to mention another factor that is common to many of the examples of awkward action. This is that often creativity is necessary and routine action is less likely to take us forward. The boxed paragraph describes an example.

A creative approach

The following example is from the last stages of the sale where things can so often stick in a "leave it with me stage". It makes the point that sometimes there is little new left to say, just "it's me again", especially if the proposition is good and the only reason for lack of confirmation is timing or distraction rather than that the customer is totally unconvinced. Then the job is to continue to maintain contact, and ultimately to jog people into action, while appearing distinctive or memorable in the process.

Following writing a short book for a specialist publisher, I was keen to undertake another topic for them in the same format. I proposed the idea and got a generally good reaction – but no confirmation. I wrote and telephoned numerous times. Nothing: just a delay or a put off (you may know the feeling!). Finally, when a reminder of the possibility came up yet again from my diary, I felt I had exhausted all the conventional possibilities, so I sat down and wrote the following:

Struggling author, patient, reliable (non-smoker), seeks commission on business topics. Novel formats preferred, but anything considered within reason; ideally 100 or so pages, on a topic like sales excellence sounds good – maybe with some illustrations. Delivery of the right quantity of material – on time – guaranteed. Contact me at the above address/telephone number or meet on neutral ground, carrying a copy of Publishing News and wearing a carnation.

I must confess I hesitated over it a little, thinking it perhaps too informal or not sufficiently businesslike (this was someone I had met only once), but, unable to think of anything better, I signed and posted it.

Gratifyingly the confirmation was received the following day (and you can read the result – *The Sales Excellence Pocketbook*, published by Management Pocketbooks). Sometimes a slightly less conventional approach works well, in part simply by standing out and being unexpected. You should not reject anything other than the conventional approach; try a little experiment and see what it can do for you

So, overall here, think of how valuable one current contact is and how easily you might never have got the train of events it involves started.

2. Managing your time

We all have to work within the constraints of the resources at our disposal. We are used to having only a finite budget, a particular level of staffing or other resources. Consider another resource: time. Somehow this is viewed differently. People who are instinctively careful about budgets and finances, squander time as if it was not a resource at all. Yet, unless there are executives in the worlds near Alpha Centuri bending their tentacles to the problem for longer, we all have to work within a 24-hour day.

This topic was given some space early on (see Chapter 2) and the details of it will not be returned to here – suffice to say that attitudes to it can be so classic that it must appear in this list. People feel – and say – that there is nothing that can be done to relieve their workload or get better organised, and do so with real conviction. But so often what they mean is – *changing my habits here needs some effort, it is difficult, so actually I will not do anything about it*. Time could be found if priorities were set well, and lack of time is simply wheeled out as an excuse for delay or inaction. The status quo, however undesirable, can so easily continues.

The discomfort trap strikes again – and in a way that affects every working hour.

3. Saying "no"

This may seem an odd example, but it very much links to time management (point 2 above). If you have too much to do then it is a fair bet that you have some things on your to do list that could have been avoided: all you had to do was to say "no" when they came up. But often that seems difficult to do.

Now I am not suggesting that you incur the wrath of your boss by refusing his next request (though there may be occasions when a firm "no" *should* be addressed to the boss, especially the boss with a hand on your knee!). I am, however, very much suggesting that you should consider saying no more often and perhaps see doing so in a fresh, positive light.

Very often this is a discomfort situation where the level of discomfort is minor, though perhaps our view of it is compounded by time considerations. We do not say no, even to things which manifestly we should not be agreeing to, because:

- it will cause an argument

- the argument will take time and cause ripples

- it will need an explanation to resolve the argument; taking more time

- it will leave you looking unhelpful, or worse, even when you are right and that can be made clear

- it may be reciprocated later when you want someone else to say "yes".

In many instances none of these things is insurmountable. Of course, you cannot go around saying an unthinking and abrupt no to all and sundry and expect that there will be no repercussions. You may well feel discomfort if you do so, and collect more tangible disadvantages too. But surely some of these can be softened. A little tact, some explanation – and a reduction in the category of negative responses you always regret not giving can be achieved. Your reputation and profile will not take a dive, you will not be thought universally unreasonable – but you will be able to focus better on your key tasks unencumbered by some of the digressions you otherwise let yourself in for with a different approach.

This is a clear example of the sorts of thing that become habits. You have people and things about which your fear of discomfort when asked to do, or become involved in, something is instinctive – you find that, even after mild protest (which people learn means nothing), you are quickly moving into an ill considered, *I suppose so.* Better to say an enthusiastic "yes" or to say, and mean, "no" where appropriate. Sometimes a "no" albeit perhaps a delayed "no", can have long-term implications. More than once I have advised clients to tackle the situation of an over-demanding (and therefore low profit) customer amidst fears that, *we'll lose their business*, and the customer has responded not only by backing down, but also by changing their ways in the long term and, in some instances, saying, *We wondered when you would raise this!* In such situations imagine behaviour twice as bad, three times as bad – would you say "no" then? There is surely a line beyond which you will not go, whatever the discomfort. The principle is easy to accept. So, maybe there are occasions when you must simply rule that line earlier; sometimes much earlier.

Curious things, habits. People themselves never know they have them.

Agatha Christie

This approach is also something that you can quickly tag as "firm change". Every time you feel yourself wanting to say "no" and wavering, pause, count to ten if it helps and then resolve to not only say it, but of make it stick.

This is one clear instance when being negative can be positive; you may well end up feeling that the occasional moment's twinge of discomfort is well worthwhile.

4. Making a presentation

This is something many people must do and it can produce major discomfort. It can be done well however. Few people are natural presenters; those that make it look easy tend to do so because they work at it. Anyone can make an acceptable, workmanlike presentation and many find that it is something at which they can excel if they go about it correctly.

But stand up totally unprepared and, oh dear, oh dear, things can go very wrong: see box.

Winging it

At worst, people stumble, they hesitate, and they sweat. They begin every other sentence with the superfluous word *"Basically"*. Commenting on some project, they say *"Um, err ... at this moment in time we are making considerable progress with the necessary preliminary work prior to the establishment of the initial first phase of work"* when they mean *"We aim to start soon"*.

Just when they should impress their audience with their expertise and confidence, and make them interested in what they have to say, they upset or confuse them. Exactly what is said and how it is put matters, indeed there may be a great deal hanging on it.

At worst, people go on too long, their explanation explains nothing and where they are going is wholly unclear. Some fidget endlessly, others remain stock still gripping the table or lectern in front of them until their knuckles go white and fear rises from them like a mist. Still others are apt to pick holes in people in the audience, or their noses. If they use slides, then they can only be read from the back of the room with a telescope, something made worse by their asking brightly *"Can you see alright at the back?"* despite the fact that there is precious little they can do about it if the answer is *"no"*, and in any case they should not be asking, they should *know* their slides are legible. They barely pause for breath, rushing from one word to the next, many of them inappropriately chosen or too long. Indeed, the only long word of which some speakers appear ignorant is rehearsal.

Of course, a lucky few believe that making a presentation is second nature. They can wing it. They are convinced that they know their stuff and how to put it over. Their first rule then, is of course to assume that the audience is somewhat thick and will, provided the right level of impenetrable gobbledegook is hit, instantly conclude that they are in the presence of a master.

Winging it means that if they want people to actually understand even the gist of what is said – some care must be taken. So, they talk v-e-r-y ... s-l-o-w-l-y; use simple words, and generally proceed on the basis that the audience have the brains of a retarded dormouse.

They spell out complicated bits in CAPITAL LETTERS, speaking more loudly as they do so, and they are careful not to be condescending, as that will upset people (you do *know* what condescending *means* don't you?).

For this kind of speaker, a presentation is something to savour. They need only the briefest of introductions and they are away, moving quickly past the first slide without noticing that it is upside down, the coins in their trouser pocket rattling at 90 decibels and the audience hanging on their every repetitive mannerism as they mutter to themselves *"If he scratches his backside whilst stood on one leg once more, I'm walking out."* It makes lesser mortals feel sadly inadequate – even the famous: it was Mark Twain who reportedly said, *"It normally takes me three weeks to prepare a good impromptu speech."* Poor man. Thankfully he was a good writer.

This (exaggerated) example points up a rather different problem about making presentation. Faced with having to make a presentation on a particular date, most people will give it some thought and be ready to stand up at the appointed time. They do, after all, recognise the pain of standing up and not being able to string one word sensibly in front of another. Certainly not all presentations go well (and often there are no marks out of ten, it either works – winning business or getting agreement of some other sort – or it is wasted).

The human brain starts working the moment you are born and never stops until you stand up to speak in public.

Sir George Jessel

In my training and consultancy work with presenters, everything from basic training to fine-tuning and rehearsal, one thing occurs repeatedly: people failing to make as good an impression as they intended admit – *I guess I did not spend sufficient time preparing.* They do not really need me to tell them this. They know preparation is key. They may well even be able to identify particular elements that preparation would have sorted; yet still they did not do enough.

This is, I believe, another aspect of the discomfort dilemma. What happens? A presentation is scheduled but time to prepare is not, or not enough. The immediate discomfort – having to rearrange activities to allow suitable preparation time, having to delay or turn down other things, perhaps having to allow other people to see how much preparation is necessary – such thoughts all end up making delaying or skimping preparation seem like *the best thing to do at the moment.*

Another factor here is a failure to accurately judge your own skills. Someone may really convince themselves they only need a few minutes to prepare, when the real situation is that, while they know preparation is necessary, they are uncertain how to go about it. Taking too short a time and muddling through takes longer and may still fail to do the necessary job. Or sometimes peoples' uncertainty relates to what it is – the right sort of presentation to meet the brief – which they are trying to prepare.

Such attitudes can be sustained for long periods (perhaps until a training course is organised!). Yet the logic is clear. In order to make a good presentation, you need to know something about what makes a presentation good and about the tricks of the trade that will allow you to plan, prepare and deliver a good one. It is unrealistic to think you can wing it, and the truth of the matter is that few people can do so, however much some good presenters may give this impression. Though experience can reduce the time preparation takes, it is usually some degree of preparation that makes a presenter seem to be "a natural", and allows them to appear to be acting effortlessly.

To quote a phrase from a training film (*I Wasn't Prepared for That*, produced by UK training film maker, Video Arts), "a presentation is the business equivalent of an open goal."

Well executed, it represents too significant an opportunity to allow discomfort to dilute it by default.

Either reason here, being unrealistic about:

- taking the necessary time for something

- the skills* you need to do something well

can apply to numbers of tasks and areas. For example, I encounter similar attitudes amongst delegates on business writing courses (and reports can often be as dire as a bad presentation – and furthermore a poor report may return to haunt you months after its submission).

Do not let a shortfall in skill (which can be rectified) lead you into inappropriate decisions dictated by the thought of discomfort.

5. Idea suggestion

If there is one area where progress is often stillborn it is in the adoption of ideas. It is less that there are insufficient new ideas, rather that they are snuffed out unconsidered – I'm sure it wouldn't work – or, because of the discomfort felt to be inherent in suggesting them, they never see the light of day in the first place.

---

* For more about the skills involved see *How to craft successful business presentations* (Patrick Forsyth, Foulsham)

> **A new idea is delicate. It can be killed by a sneer or a yawn; it can be stabbed to death by a quip and worried to death by a frown on the right man's brow.**
>
> *Charles Bower*

The quotation above says it all. Yet how often have you decided to bite your tongue and not to say something for fear of rejection? I wonder what significant, positive differences there might be now in your organisation if you had tackled the discomfort and spoken out. Ideas do not care who has them, and managers should not care either. A manager is not paid to have all the ideas that are necessary to keep their operation up to date and forging ahead, but they are paid to somehow ensure that there are sufficient ideas to keep things moving ahead. The wise manager will encourage ideas from wherever they can, especially from around their team.

But ... there is always a but. Realistically not all ideas will be welcomed with open arms in even the best-organised organisation. It is the nature of things that some will prove less than ideal; though one thing can lead to another and discussion prompted by an unacceptable idea may well lead to a better and more appropriate one being adopted. Besides as we are each different in our skills, experience and so on and thus have a different perspective on things, sometimes a fresh pair of eyes as it were can cast new light on something. This can produce ideas that others are too close to see and can thus contribute usefully in a way that would not otherwise occur. So:

Ideas may not automatically be greeted with open arms, but they should always be greeted with open minds.

So, what do you do if you have a "good idea"? You should:

- think about it yourself before you mention it to anyone (this may be extensive or simply a moment's thought before you speak out in a meeting)

- test it if possible (a trial run, a word with a colleague acting as a sounding board, for instance)

- consider it in the round, including long and short term and the implications far and wide (it is possible for an idea to improve one immediate area and yet not fit more broadly)

- then, if it seems worth real consideration, make the suggestion, and do so with conviction

- recognise in so doing that the best you can hope for is a good strike rate – not all your ideas will be worth taking up, but some will and you may well gain a good reputation as an ideas person without having a one hundred percent strike rate.

It is easy to say, "suggest it", but doing so might take several forms. It might only necessitate a few words at a meeting; though they should be well chosen ones. It might mean a well-reasoned and well-documented case being made – persuasively – in a written report. Whatever is done it must be well executed, it must not fail the idea merely by making an inadequate case for it. Worth thinking about – creativity is an essential part of many management jobs.

Open-mindedness is a necessary partner here if you are on the receiving end of idea suggestions. It is important that your instinctive reaction is not negative and perhaps based as much as anything on your own view being challenged or bettered. So don't say to yourself, *What on earth would they know about this?* Or voice out loud an immediate reservation, *That's no good.* Think about it and concentrate on the solution it might provide rather than any discomfort acceptance of something might cause.

Creativity is never easy; so never let a creative input become impossible because making it may be uncomfortable.

Incidentally, creativity is necessary in every environment. The pressures of corporate life can stifle it – *there's no time just to think!* But many people are very creative given the chance (and chance can become habit). In conducting training courses, for instance for such bodies as management institutes, I notice that in syndicate work for example, people can be very creative; yet here, as elsewhere in the world, they sometimes comment on the difficulty of doing the same within their own company.

6. Dealing with poor performance

For those who manage others this is a classic. I am sure you do not surround yourself with incompetents, but over time and with a number of people reporting to you this does crop up. Indeed it may do so simply as a result of change: jobs move on, make new demands and suddenly someone is no longer doing what is really required of them to be effective.

This is also something that engenders classic people orientated discomfort. Only the sadists enjoy saying to someone that they are not pulling their weight. Only the chronically insecure will not respond defensively – that is a reflex – so challenging poor performance seems a sure way to an argument or resentment. So, what does happen? Too often we convince ourselves that the short fall in performance is temporary – a blip. It will get better soon. Leave well alone, wait for next month's figures (or till year end, after the holiday – when the cows come home). The most common delay – coupled of course with a firm decision to tackle it head on – is to decide to wait for something specific (anything) coupled with an, often irrational, belief that *it will get better*. Maybe it will. More often it needs addressing in a positive way.

Consider the situation objectively:

- The results orientation of most jobs and organisations demand that such a situation is not left.

- There are other reasons, the motivation of the rest of a team who see a passenger in their midst amongst others, that demand action.

- The outcome is, by definition positive: an improvement (one the poor performer will regard positively if it is well handled).

- The analysis and action are not complicated.

That being so, why does poor performance tend to be allowed to continue for too long? In a word because dealing with it is difficult and felt to engender – discomfort. This may not be true. It surely should be the case that any employee knows what performance is required of them and that they are thus aware when their performance is slipping. If so, the problem being addressed will not come as a surprise to them; they will expect it to need dealing with. In many circumstances the outcome will be positive all round – better performance and someone ultimately reassured that they are back on track. Only if such things are not regularly and constructively addressed will people respond badly to the one occasion when something is done.

Failure is the opportunity to begin again more intelligently.

Henry Ford

The options for action are, in any case, few. When faced with poor performance there are only three things you can do:

1   Put up with it; which is not to be recommended
2   Correct it, so that satisfactory performance occurs in future
3   Remove the person from the job and replace them with someone who can perform to standard (this might mean rearranging work allocation and moving a task, moving the poor performer to different work or terminating their employment).

Addressing the correction of performance is again conceptually straightforward. Either the person is:

- able to perform as you want, but is not doing so

- not able to do what is required of them.

In the first case, you may need to apply discipline and/or motivation, and initially, of course, it is sensible to ascertain why the lapse is occurring: have they taken their eye off the ball, do they have a problem at home – or what? In the second case you need to develop them so that they can do better, and this, as has been said, may be necessary only because of some change in circumstances affecting their job; like increased use of computers. Such a change may be unexpected, external and mean there is no reflection on the staff member for not having the ideal current level of skill.

The time to take further action, to remove the person, is when action has been taken to correct matters (and sufficient time allowed for change) and no improvement is forthcoming. The timing is important, it may take a while for someone to become adept at something new, for instance, and there may be other delays even when the cause has been identified; for example a slot may need to be found for someone to attend a training course.

Note: if, as occasionally happens, the problem can only be reconciled with a drastic solution then this too must be addressed promptly. The most difficult option is firing people. Such action needs the mandatory preliminary of a careful checking of procedure and of employment legislation (the latter, it should be noted, is becoming ever more complex and of course varies country by country around the world). Beyond that the action needs taking and taking promptly. The decision may have in a sense to be ruthless, but it is always the best policy (and good public relations) to sever employment on as fair, amicable and generous a basis as possible.

There may be many forms of remedial action possible, but the sequence and principle of action described here is clear. So too are the penalties of taking no action and leaving poor performance to continue: just imagine it in terms of any job for which you are responsible. For example, beyond the question of the individual, motivation is affected throughout a team; people resent passengers, especially if it means doing more work to make up for it.

It is worth noting too that the situation is similar with regard to a range of staff performance issue, rather than simply overall results achieved. These include:

- Poor timing keeping. This can reduce productivity and affect results and can also cause de-motivation and resentment; at worst, it can set a bad example other people follow

- Poor discipline. Not following rules or standard procedures can cause similar problems, indeed such can cause worse problems (if ignoring a rule puts the organisation in breach of something like employment legislation)

- Interpersonal relationships where either good ones – a romance – or bad ones – a feud – amongst staff can cause problems, which are also best dealt with promptly and decisively; though the examples do not demand the same action.

You can probably think of many more such instances (indeed we continue the theme in point 7 next); all, despite the obvious benefits of dealing with them, and the equally obvious penalties of delay or inaction, pose difficulty and are all too apt to create immediate discomfort that results in less than effective decisions and handling of the problem.

A little action soon – a stitch in time, if you like – is always going to be better than a delay and then real drama and greater difficulty.

The next section links in here and looks at confrontational situations generally and may add something to what has been said here.

7. Confrontational situations

Some problems combine factors in a way that enhances their potential difficulty. Such may be exceptional, but involve conflict between people, which may be potential or actual. One example is the breaking of rules. Sometimes this may be straightforward, as with poor timekeeping, which is simple to the extent that someone is either in late or not (though the validity of the reasons for it may be difficult to judge). On other occasions it may be less clear, as with a less than well-described office dress code that needs some subjective interpretation.

In all such cases there is the threat of argument and a defensive response if you broach it with the perpetrator. Discomfort rears its head again; confrontation is not high on most managers' list of favourite things. So there are plenty of reasons to let things ride. You:

- hope something is an isolated incident and will not reoccur

- hope that something will prompt change without your intervention (others muttering about bad timekeeping, say)

- think there is a chance of action making things worse.

There is also the skills problem. If the matter is exceptional – as something like bullying or discrimination hopefully is, for example – then you may have no prior experience of what to do. Putting yourself in a position to know what to do is going to take time and effort, and being busy provides a seemingly "good" reason to put that off.

Other factors can compound these difficulties. Maybe the person you need to address about such behaviour is older or more experienced than you are, maybe a difference in gender makes things more stressful (despite the politically correct and fair society we are now supposed to inhabit). Other factors can compound the problem; for instance, in Asia the concept of "losing face" can also be of influence here. For these reasons and more some things really do suggest major discomfort to come. So, what to do?

First it should be said that dealing with such things is made immeasurably easier by clear, well spelt out guidelines and consistency of practice. If you let things go half the time, especially if the rules have an element of ambiguousness about them, then you can confidently expect a greater level of confrontation when you do pick up on someone (and they will certainly see it as picking on them if you make them the exception).

Secondly, secrecy – unnecessary secrecy – compounds the problem, tending to create confrontation and difficulty based on what people think is the case about something, rather than the facts. As an example, I know of one company where all salaries are public knowledge. If anyone wants to know what someone else earns they can go into the accountant's office and ask. This is primarily a control on those managers setting salaries to do so fairly. If Mr A is earning more than Ms B, then there better be a good reason. The result is a well-administered salary scale and virtually no rumour, hassle or upset about it. This is not recommended for every organisation (the one in question had a staff of about a hundred people) of course, and may be an extreme example, but it makes a good point – and might even be a good idea for some.

Thirdly, it is things of this sort about which the following maxim could not be more true:

If you leave a difficult problem then it becomes, not easier, but more difficult; and rarely, if ever, does it go away.

Delay can have further negative results. For instance, if you do not deal with a case of bullying, then the person bullied may raise it at a higher level. You will then not only have to sort it out with someone else watching to see how well you handle it, but also have to explain why it was not dealt with promptly in the first place; and this could be at a tribunal.

Yes, there is unavoidable discomfort in some things that must be dealt with, but it must be done. When you see this sort of trouble on the horizon always remind yourself not of the pain of dealing with it now, but of the greater pain all round of dealing with it later.

8. Job appraisal interviews

Many mangers take appraising their staff very seriously. It is, after all, a significant opportunity to ensure good performance in the coming period and to set up any matters, for example development, that will enhance its likelihood. But, there are also many managers (most, dare I say?) who find the whole process very awkward. The result is people who find that what should be an important event in the year is awkward for them too and, worse, offers no practical benefit or satisfaction. This seems to be true wherever in the world I go.

So, here is an example of pending discomfort that affects activity throughout the year. Appraisals, well-conducted appraisals, do not just happen. They are the culmination of a whole series of planning and activities that must take place on a considered, ongoing basis through the year. The awkwardness is often, in my experience, due to uncertainty about how to conduct such a meeting well. The trouble is that if the matter is down-graded from the beginning because of this overall feeling of discomfort, then the necessary preliminary processes are omitted or skimped. As a result, come the day it is almost impossible to do justice to the meeting and failure becomes a self-fulfilling prophecy. The moral?

Do not end up trading avoiding some discomfort early on in a process for a double ration at a later date.

The correct handling of job appraisal meetings is too broad a topic to review in detail here, key pointers do, however, appear in the next, largely checklist-style section.

Key issues in conducting job appraisals successfully

Some care is necessary. For instance, it is worth any appraiser bearing in mind that:

• the meeting and the agenda should be set up well in advance (and any necessary documentation read or otherwise dealt with ahead of the meeting)

• adequate time must be allowed (on the basis that results will make it time well spent)

• surroundings must be comfortable and interruptions must be prevented

• all those involved must be in agreement about the format and the practicality of the proceedings

• documentation and any element of "scoring" must be clear ahead of the meeting

• targets and other objectives relevant to the period under review must be on the table, every aspect of the appraisal must deal with facts (no one should be making judgements on hearsay or uncertain memory)

• discussion must be open, judgements objective and everyone open minded

• it should be recognised that listening is as important as talking

Both parties should resolve to deal with sensitive issues, not allow peer embarrassment to sideline them (criticism is part of appraisal, though it must be constructively given and received and lead to change if necessary).

In addition, two overriding principles are paramount. It is in the nature of a successful appraisal that:

- the appraisee does most of the talking (though the appraiser may need to chair and direct the meeting)

- the focus, and weight of time and discussion, is on the future more than about the past (the two go together, of course, but the end results are action for the future, albeit stemming, in part, from the experience of the period just gone).

Approached in the right way this is one of management's greatest opportunities to create good future performance.

Note: this is such an important area, and so many people are unsatisfied with their own appraisals that it is worth adding a little about getting the most from being appraised. This too may be worried about, but no preparation be done before the interview; something else that may seem difficult and uncomfortable. So, at the risk of digression, let's consider three areas about appraisals for a moment.

1. Preparing for them

Be sure you understand how the appraisal system in your organisation works before you find yourself in such a meeting. Before your first such meeting you are likely to need more detailed information than once you are into the routine. So, first time round, ask for information if this is not provided and ask some of your longer serving peers how their meetings go, how long they last and what they get from them. Particularly be sure you know why appraisals are done, how management conducting them views them, what they look to get from them, and what time span the review covers.

Then you can consider how you want the meeting to go and how you can influence it. For instance ask yourself what:

- you want to raise and discuss

- is likely to be raised (and responses to any negative areas that may come up)

- the link is between appraisal and, development and training and what you hope to get in this area

- the link is between the meeting and your future work, responsibilities and projects undertaken

- questions you want to ask

If it is not your first appraisal, check what was said at, and documented after, the last one. This must be done in the context of what you now know about the forthcoming appraisal meeting. A couple of points are worth careful planning:

- One is the link to salary review and other benefits. Many organisations separate discussion of this from appraisal meetings (indeed there is a strong case for doing so), if this is the case then salary cannot be raised, except perhaps in general terms. If it will be discussed you may have things to prepare (and calculate) here also.

- Another key point is the make-up of the discussion in terms of time scale. As has been said, a good appraisal will always spend more time on the future than on the past, both aspects need thought and certainly there is no excuse for your not having the facts at your fingertips about anything that is a likely candidate for discussion in the review of past events.

Make notes as you plan, and take them with you to the meeting – there is no point in trusting to memory and, in any case, being seen to have thought seriously about the meeting will benefit you. You may only get one, sometimes two, such opportunities in any single year. Therefore, some careful preparation will prevent the occasion being wasted.

2. During the interview

The person who is conducting the appraisal will have a bearing on both how it is done and how you need to conduct yourself. If it is with a manager with whom you are on good terms and see every day, this will make for a less formal meeting than if it is someone more senior with whom you only have occasional contact (some appraisals involve three people including the person to be appraised).

A good appraisal will:

- be notified well in advance

- have clear agenda

- have a particular duration in mind.

And so these are things you should ask for if necessary. Particularly you may want to have ideas about how much time will be spent discussing last year and next, how interactive the meeting is and when you can ask questions, perhaps also what is, and is not, on the record. Some appraisals are rather checklist in style: that is the appraiser leads the conversation and raises the points one at a time, asking for your view or comment. Others are more open and allow the person being appraised to lead, pulling them back to an agenda only if the meeting digresses too much. Ideally you will know which way it runs, but you must be ready for either. Remember lack of comment may be read as lack of awareness, knowledge or as indecisiveness. On the other hand, if the question posed needs some thought then it is better to let the appraiser know rather than answering with a hasty comment.

Appraisals should not be traumatic occasions. If they are constructive – and prompting positive change in the future is the only real reason for doing them – then you can take a reasonably relaxed view of them (provided you have done some preparation) and there is no reason why you should not enjoy as well as find them useful. You are on show, career planning decisions are being made, albeit long term, by those conducting these meetings, but it is also a positive opportunity for you to present something of your competence in a way that goes "on the record".

3. Follow up

Appraisals are too important to just file away in your mind or forget about once they are past. They can provide a catalyst to an ongoing dialogue during the year. In many organisations, the system demands that the appraiser documents proceedings, and usually that the appraisee confirms that this documentation is a true record of the salient issues.

But there is no reason why you cannot take the initiative on particular matters. Consider the following as an example. Development requirements are a common topic that most appraisals review. This may result in specific action – *I will enrol you on that communication course next month* – or it may result in further discussion, more than can be accommodated in the appraisal meeting itself. It may be useful to volunteer to undertake the processes involved (remember your boss could have a dozen appraisals in the same week and much attendant administration). If you put in a paper setting out some suggestions for action, and if this is used as the agenda for another session about it, then this could well see more of what you plan to happen happening, and happening sooner, than would otherwise be the case. Similarly use the opportunity to report back after any agreed training, in writing or at a meeting, so that the dialogue continues. If the training has been agreed as successful then there is logic in discussing "what's next".

A final point – you may think attending them is a chore, but appraisals are not easy to conduct, take time to prepare and always seem to be scheduled during busy periods. So, if it has been useful, express thanks and if it has not, try to comment in a way that may set the scene for a more productive encounter – and less discomfort – next time.

9. Positive use of rules

All managers these days are surely well aware that management is not simply about telling people what to do. Consultation in all its forms is the order of the day. The problem (again) is time. What do you consult about and what do you not? Consultation is more than a mechanism to solicit agreement to action. It can also be an essentially creative process and should prompt ideas – everything from new ways of doing things to new things to do.

That being so action is necessary to make sufficient time available for consultation whenever it is advantageous to do so. You cannot discuss everything, and one way to avoid issues being inappropriately time consuming is to have, and stick to, some good operational rules. In other words there should be some things people simply take as givens, accept and do not argue about – with the compensating benefit that it is seen as clearing the way for other, more useful, consultation and feedback.

Making and sticking to rules is another classic discomfort area. It has to be well considered and appropriate; and ensuring this is so takes time. There is the worry that rules will be thought draconian, cause resentment and that sorting that out will waste more time. The trick is to make good rules and explain them clearly; and to do so not only individually in terms of their sense or necessity, but also in terms of saving time.

People actually like to know the ground rules. They like to "know where they are". But if things are not clear, then anarchy can rule – and the time taken up with pleadings of special circumstances, exceptions and precedents runs riot. Avoidance of constant query, or unrest, is just one reason why rules should be fair, if possible.

> **The golden rule is that there are no golden rules.**
>
> *George Bernard Shaw*

One of the examples of this, which I like and which well illustrates the principle here, concerns a field sales team (though the principle could apply in many ways). Renown for hating admin, external sales people tend to be dilatory about filling in reports, forms and the like. In one company the rule was established that unless every form (there were only half a dozen or so) was in on time at the end of the month, and was complete and legible – then the form designed to record expenses and trigger repayment (something that was never late!) was delayed until the following month.

The effect was revolutionary. Suddenly administration was completed properly. The monthly time-consuming chore of chasing those who were late (in a situation where information had to be consolidated and was useless until everyone had submitted it), returning things that were incomplete and waiting again for their return – all ceased. The time saved was significant. To make the rule acceptable, time was given to other issues the team wanted addressed, and that time was labelled as available because of their more disciplined behaviour. I know of a number of organisations that operate similar policies successfully.

The point here is that this was quickly accepted and worked well – as can be many other similarly sensible rules (which makes the point that rules must be reviewed regularly and kept up to date; anything which time and change renders inappropriate will do more harm than good). The creation such may seem difficult, but a moment in the discomfort zone leads you to a situation where actually future difficulty that would otherwise be ongoing is reduced or removed.

Seeming uncertainty and difficulty can be turned into something positive, changing both how things are seen and done.

10. Powerful people

Finally, an example designed to show that discomfort may well come, and be as tangible, not from what you have to do, but from the circumstances in which you have to do it. Dealing with someone senior – and daunting – is a good example of exactly that.

Maybe it is the boss. Maybe it is someone else from the higher reaches of the organisation. Either may be made more daunting by reputation – though this may compare less than accurately with reality – or imagination.

The discomfort of having to deal with an unknown quantity is, nevertheless, real. Above all rejection is probably the commonest fear. This may just be a fear of their irritation – *they don't have time for me* – or of an idea being rejected and the encounter tarring you with a brush that ensures future encounters are worse – *they'll never take me seriously again.*

Because of all such feelings the now well described fear of discomfort and thus inaction follows. Things are put off, ideas are left pending and then forgotten and instead of working actively to create and maintain good relations with such people, the perceived difficulty means that a significantly important area of work activity is in danger of being ignored as part of what could make you effective and help achieve objectives.

I don't want yes-men around me. I want everybody to tell me the truth – even if it costs them their job.

Film producer Sam Goldwyn

It is perhaps worth noting in passing that bosses can contribute to or create this feeling in others. It is a sure sign of a poor manager if their team assume any summons, especially an urgent one, automatically means something is wrong. If the majority of contacts are positive and constructive, then this feeling will not be engendered – it's something for everyone who manages others to think on.

So, how does one avoid an uncomfortable feeling when dealing with the senior and powerful? Two things are key:

- **The person.** Be sure that your dealings are based on a factual view of the person. Ignore the rumours and beware of false impressions and untypical precedents; just because someone was short with you once does not mean that they will never make time for you in the future. So find out about them and let the facts dictate the way you deal with things.

- **Their methods.** Similarly try to understand something of how they work. They are busy; and they may have many people reporting to and in touch with them. What does this mean? That they appreciate good use of time, getting to the point promptly, a clear brief and matters being handled the way they want. For example, in a meeting they may give you a specific time – *Okay, let's hear it, you've got ten minutes.* The response to this must not be to struggle and fail to keep to it, doing no justice to what you have to say. You have to respect it. By all means negotiate it, by all means limit what you try to do in it – *Right, in that time let me just describe this and this* – but make sure they know they are getting a considered and appropriate response and not a panic-stricken one.

Note: if in doubt *ask* (often a simple question – again something that can be ducked – brings a simple straightforward answer, causes no hassle and makes everything easier and more certain). Alternatively, you can do some checking.

If you are an effective person, if you act on the basis of some thought and logic, then there is no reason why you cannot deal with a few seemingly scary people as well as you deal with any others.

> ***Do not let the smokescreen of false information or assumption create difficulty and discomfort where none should exist.***

With these specific examples in mind, we now turn to the wider picture and how the right approach can provide many more opportunities to avoid discomfort traps and make action more effective.

More opportunities

Once the reflex of truly considering something with a view to action, and in the knowledge that this is truly preferable to allowing it to be sidelined by default, is established, then you can usefully comb incoming tasks and situations for this opportunity.

Every time you get to grips with something essentially uncomfortable, and manage in the discomfort zone, you are likely to improve performance and results compared with those accruing if you allow avoidance of discomfort to rule the day. You need a maxim (rather as in George Orwell's "Animal Farm" – Four legs good, two legs bad): discomfort is, if not good, a likely and regular route to action and improved performance. It is literally something to be sought and embraced because of what it can achieve.

This principle, as we have seen, can be applied to matters arising only occasionally. For example:

- **Staff recruitment.** Sometimes the following can occur. You hit an impasse; having been through the whole process of finding and interviewing candidates there is no one that is ideal. Do you hire the best of a bad bunch, or do you bite the discomfort bullet and seek additional candidates to take the process further and get the right candidate who will really do the job well? The results of appointing an inappropriate or weak candidate are dire, yet the discomfort and inconvenience of going through the whole process again weighs heavy. Further, being short staffed can make matters worse, the pressure to appoint no matter what is intense (especially in certain high employment areas). This is an example of something that, while it may not occur too often, has far reaching repercussions if we get it wrong

- **Staff promotion.** In a situation where good performance merits promotion, a situation that is surely wholly positive and likely to have both motivational and performance benefits wider than the individual, a discomfort trap may still loom. Maybe it is just that we are busy and changes will take up time. Maybe an increase in salary that must accompany promotion seems "better" delayed to a later budget period. Again dangers are evident and possible sidelining is to be avoided.

Additionally, there are a host of small, and perhaps seemingly unimportant, issues where the discomfort trap can act to change what we select to do. For example, you may:

- decline to make a comment (perhaps a rebuttal) at a meeting because you are unprepared and unsure what to say. If you let the moment pass what are the consequences? And are they likely to lead to greater discomfort?

- omit confirming something in writing, because it would need a lengthy document or just be a chore, and then find a greater problem with misunderstandings that occur as a result.

- fail to learn from a mistake because you bury it without analysis or thought in order to move on and so that others do not know about it.

There are very many things of this sort: many occur regularly, often, or both

Think positive, watch for opportunities and develop the habit of tackling the uncomfortable as a priority.

You may find there are innumerable occasions when what you do can be viewed in this sort of way. Finding them may be no great problem, but take heed of the philosophy expressed in the quotation below:

The truth of the matter is that you always know the right thing to do. The hard part is doing it.

General Norman Schwarzkoff

Once upon a time (continued)

The lion was indeed irritated by the wolf's unannounced interruption, but he was in a mellow mood and rejected a violent response. So, he paused and gave it a moment's thought. You should become a bunny rabbit, said the lion, *everyone loves a bunny rabbit, I think it's the long floppy ears and the big eyes. Yes, that's it – become a bunny rabbit.* The wolf did the wolf equivalent of touching his forelock, thanked the lion profusely and slunk away. He had an answer.

To be continued …

$$\overline{\underline{5}}$$

Planning to change

If in the last few years you haven't discarded a major opinion or acquired a new one, check your pulse. You may be dead.

Gelett Burgess

Though it is said that nothing makes you more productive than the last minute, it is a basic – and sensible – premise of efficient working to ensure that you assess your own situation, and actively take steps to deploy your working time and effort in such a way as will best help you achieve what you want.

Such an approach highlights the whole area of personal time management. The principles of this were touched on earlier and are not complex. Rather they are wholly logical, but success is in the detail and this is a topic that it is beyond the brief here to go into further.

Tomorrow is always the busiest day of the week.

Jonathon Lazear

One principle is worth restating here however: the truth that self-organisation does not just happen, it needs thought, organisation and time. It is time pressure that makes many people less organised than they might be or want to be. The tyranny of the urgent makes pausing to consider such issues seem like an indulgence.

It is not.

Time invested wisely can save time later, and the logical outturn of the review prompted by this book is a case in point. If your reading of this book leads on to the establishment of a powerful, positive habit – that of recognising your possible negative response to potential difficulty and to a specific resolve to grasp the nettle and manage in the discomfort zone – then it can literally change your life. Even if you only fail currently to address a small number of uncomfortable situations as perhaps you should, just the benefits of changing your approach to those could be substantial. One new idea successfully sold to colleagues (or the boss or board), one new contact that could so easily not have been made, one member of your staff nudged to an improvement in their skill or performance, in every case overall results feel the benefit. In some cases what can occur is not a momentary gain, but a gain that is made repeatedly and regularly. The more separate areas can be improved the greater the overall results gain. There is a potential here that must not be ignored.

So, having spent some time to read this far, let me encourage you to take a moment longer to focus specifically on your own situation.

Addressing the particular

To work at and address situations and tasks that are, or seem, initially uncomfortable you need to have a clear view of where possible trouble lies in your own work life. Each of us is different, not only in the roles and job we have and what those demand we do, but in our background and experience. It is largely the past that makes us susceptible to particular discomforts. I am sure that psychologists could trace, maybe back to childhood, what makes someone particularly dislike certain situations, in the way that a childhood shyness might make one person less adept at networking than someone else. In one sense the reasons matter little, certainly compared to addressing matters in the here and now.

So, to find an individual way forward you need to be clear about certain things and find a basis on which to experiment as a first step to changing habits. If you actively and consciously try a new approach, then making it work will encourage you to extend it further. Very soon the positive effects may be noticeable and considerable, and a new method of approach will become second nature. The potential here really is revolutionary. The process of addressing your own situation in this context includes:

- **Reference to your job description.** If only because of employment legislation most people these days have a job description (though there are better reasons to have and use one). This is not only a base reference for Personnel departments, it is, or should be, a working document, one that helps focus day to day activity and priorities. A check will quickly show if it is up to date, complete and clear. If not, then separate action needs to be taken to correct it. Then it provides a first guide to areas of action. Be careful if you short cut this step, most people have a breadth of responsibilities that takes a moment to call to mind, reference to a job description puts the overall picture in front of you at a stroke. It should be looked at alongside:

- **Your current "to-do" list.** Whatever form this may take it will somehow show current and future tasks and projects. Amongst these are potential discomfort traps, things in danger of being postponed, sidelined or skimped in terms of action and where a more positive approach will pay dividends. This list enables you to select a task for experiment.

If you spot something in limbo (actually or about to be; be honest, there is surely something) use it as an example:

Pick something you view as difficult in some way, with clear discomfort elements to it, and think about it in a way that enables you to list both the good effects of dealing with it promptly and well, and the negative results of leaving it unresolved.

The wide range of results

For example, if you were to select the poor performance of a member of your team, a matter touched on earlier, you could list what the results of addressing and changing it would include:

- an improvement in performance (be specific and list all the ways in which this might be measured: speed, accuracy, revenue generated – whatever)

- an avoidance of the worse problems to which continuing poor performance might lead

- an opportunity for personal development (for instance extending a skill the standard of which might have been diluting performance)

- the possibility of extending someone's range of responsibilities in light of the improved skill

- an opportunity for positive personal motivation (because development, constructively done, is always motivational)

- an opportunity for positive team motivation (as has been said, no one in a group likes passengers, and if development is available that is seen as good for everyone)

- the clearing of any unpleasant atmosphere engendered around the team by the problem not being addressed as a positive motivational effect kicks in

- a positive improvement in image (either of your department within the organisation or outside too, certainly if performance affects customers)

- an increase in positive ongoing management communication and counselling useful to the individual and appreciated by the whole team

- a boost to your own performance (you are doubtless judged not only on what you do, but also how your team operates).

Perhaps you can extend such a list: certainly you might add longer-term factors such as a contribution to staff retention, or add the ability to focus on and get done some key job itself delayed by the problem. You might also want to add the reward of a certain personal satisfaction that comes from seeing a problem well resolved. Similarly you could list the penalties of inaction: from ongoing and deteriorating performance and motivation to sanctions from above.

> **It's not whether you get knocked down, it's whether you get up.**
>
> *Vince Lombardi*

It is certainly worth noting that such lists may be long. The ramifications of some problems may extend far and wide – perhaps worryingly far and wide. However, it would be wrong to get hung up on the word "problem". Other examples might be much more positive. Someone might sideline making presentations, worrying that their skill in making them is inadequate, but might be well aware of the many advantages of being able to do them with sufficient clarity and clout. As an old proverb has it:

Behind every problem there is an opportunity – all you have to do is recognise the fact.

Analyse the chosen situation

Having selected an example, then take stock. Ask:

- What are the reasons for not addressing it (or why you do so with circumspection or unease)?

- Are the reasons practical (like the lack of being sure what to do or how to do it) or emotional (just seeming unpleasant or difficult)?

- If practical, then what steps are indicated to get over the hurdle (as in training in presentational skills)?

If the pressure is psychological, maybe it needs no more than identifying – *I know I am being silly about this* – then all that may be necessary is an act of will. Just do it, as Nike say. More likely the check will throw up some necessary preliminary action. This could take real time and effort, as if you schedule attendance on a presentations skills course. But it may be comparatively simple. You need only check a reference, have a word with a colleague or access some guidelines as to how to proceed. It could only need a moment's careful consideration. Additionally, maybe you need to consider method, or maybe you only need to think about manner – you know how to address the poor performance question, say, but want to do so in a way that comes across as motivational rather than negative.

In any event you should take the necessary preliminary action first before proceeding with the test. If you pitch into something, determined to address it head on, but still unsure how to make it work, the danger is that it will not only be distinctly uncomfortable, but that the situation will not be resolved either. Discomfort will increase, probably attended by your kicking yourself because you knew the likely outcome. In the poor performance example, fear of causing resentment and denial and of making matters worse are probably prime amongst the reasons for taking it slow.

Forearmed and appropriately equipped in terms of knowledge and skill as to how best to tackle it there is every reason to believe that all will go well. At best you will find yourself wondering why you ever saw it as a major discomfort trap in the first place.

With such an exercise gone through very consciously your ability to enter the discomfort zone and emerge not only unscathed, but also victorious, will be well demonstrated. Good, so far; what next?

> **Courage is very important. Like a muscle, it is strengthened by use.**
>
> *Ruth Gordon*

Creating a positive habit

The next step is to do more and to create circumstances that allow you to see this and similar situations differently in future. You need to:

- keep the problem in mind; keep your discomfort zone spotting antenna tuned in

- stop looking for the "easy way", especially stop pretending that an easy way will appear in time if you just wait long enough

- stop feeling inadequate about your situation. You are normal. Everyone is subject to the discomfort trap – though not everyone breaks out of it

- avoid rating yourself in negative terms – be confident and believe you can do what you want (or do what will enable you to do what you want)

- actively reject past negative influences that may have led you into the discomfort trap; that was then, this is now.

Two things together can ensure you tackle things in the discomfort zone and win.

First, the right attitude: it really does help to think in the way described above, rather than allowing an unfounded rationalisation to lead you into simply acting to avoid any looming discomfort.

Secondly, this is very much an area where experience boosts morale and a commitment to do more. After all we all know in our heart of hearts that our approach to some things is less than positive – seeing such areas resolved satisfactorily is almost bound to be a catalyst to more, similar, action.

An experiment was suggested above, one task approached in full awareness of its potential discomfort and with every intention of working through it. If you are successful, then promptly go on and try something else in the same way. If it is not successful, pause, ask why and go on to the next experiment in light of what it has taught you. Repeated attempts to break out of the trap are likely to succeed (the story included below is an appealing version of the *'if at first you don't succeed...'* proverb and makes a point worth noting).

Interlude

A now famous operatic singer was invited to perform at a major gala concert in Italy, something that was a wonderful opportunity very early in his career. He was thrilled to be there and flattered to find that, having sung his particular aria, he was called back for several encores. He said as much to the stage manager as he pushed him out onto stage again for the fourth time. "No, no Senor," he was told, "Here in Italy, I am afraid they will ask you to sing it again and again – until you get it right!"

Some things fall into a pattern. Find a way through one and you can deal with them all. Others are essentially one-off. So be it, they need individual thought, planning and execution – but the successful approach evolved in this way can be applied elsewhere. Of course, some discomfort traps may be caused by a significant gap of some sort in you or your competencies; a skill that needs enhancing is a good example. Once addressed, however, the same principle applies – the more future tasks you will be in a position to address in a straightforward and positive way.

The action lies with you. As much as anything, this book is addressed to successful managers. It shows that, however experienced and effective you are, you can likely find ways of enhancing your achievements.

It's what you learn after you know it all that counts.

John Wooden

The approaches described here are ones that not only can potentially enhance results and do so fast, they can substantially improve your job satisfaction along the way. Only not taking advantage of these opportunities is really an uncomfortable thought.

The personal dimension

The emphasis throughout the preceding pages has been on ensuring good performance, using an acceptance of discomfort to allow you to deal with difficult matters in a way, and at a time, that produces positive productivity, and creates effectiveness and efficiency as a result. This approach helps you achieve your job objectives and can be applied almost whatever the level of difficulty something (apparently) presents.

It also does more; and what else it does may provide an additional incentive to help you grasp the discomfort nettle. It works to enhance your personal profile – and thus your career prospects.

Whatever you want to do, the career the path you take, and the progress you make along it, are influenced by many things. Much is down to you. And the work environment is not automatically on your side. You have doubtless noticed that the corporate jungle is decidedly competitive these days, and an active approach to managing your career is not an option for those who want to succeed – it is much better regarded as a necessity. What is most important?

> ***You are judged by what you achieve***
> ***and by the profile you project.***

One thing is worth mentioning here. You need to be efficient. For example, I am pathological about hitting writing deadlines; it matters, it is noticed – be late and some editors will never willingly commission an author again. It is not enough to be an effective manager. Appearances matter too. If your office permanently looks as if a typhoon hit it yesterday, it may be difficult to claim at a meeting that you are confident of hitting a tight deadline; especially if you appear uncertain and disorganised at the meeting too. It is said that *'Perception is reality'* in such circumstances. You may be the most efficient person in the world, but it has to *seem* so, too, for you to reap the full reward for so being.

In case you are likely to underestimate this fact, let me give an example linked to presentations, which were used as an example earlier. I once attended a conference with speakers seated in a row across the top table on a raised platform. As I think the third speaker was introduced he stood up next to the Chair and began: "Good morning Ladies and Gentlemen, I am going to be speaking to you about ...and in the hour I have available I would like to ..." At this point the Chair reached up and tugged his sleeve. The speaker bent down and they whispered together for just a moment. The speaker then stood erect and continued: "I am so sorry Ladies and Gentlemen, in the half hour I have available ..." As this was said he tore the papers he held lengthways down the middle and threw half over his shoulder, continuing without pause apparently with just half his notes in front of him. It was clearly contrived. It had nothing at all to do with the topic, but I was impressed and, glancing round, every single one of the two hundred faces in the audience seemed to be thinking: *Now this one should be good.*

If something so disassociated from the job in hand can enhance image so much – in this case by projecting a high level of confidence – what effect can other things have? Be clear: image, and what people assume because of it, matters.

So, everything discussed here is relevant to your career progress. It helps your performance and perception to:

- consistently hit deadlines

- tackle what others perceive as difficult issues head on and make them work

- be confident of your abilities and projected performance

- have a team that do likewise.

All these, and more, have a greater likelihood of being the case if you are able to manage in the discomfort zone. Not only does every delayed or avoided issue risk diluting your performance, it is likely to dilute your image too. If when opportunities present themselves you can be a natural choice, working to achieve this is surely very much part of active career management. It will help you and your employer alike, in both the short and the long term.

Weaving a net is better than praying for fish.

Chinese proverb

An example is provided by a delegate who attended a public seminar I conducted on one occasion on the topic of business writing. As is the way with such events, everyone introduced themselves. When I asked this person why they were attending he said simply, I'm missing out. I asked him to explain what he meant, and he said that he knew that his boss would not involve him in any project that involved writing a report; his were too dire. He had to improve this skill if he was to progress. At that moment he hated writing reports, he delayed it, rushed it and – by wallowing in the discomfort – effectively made it impossible to succeed at it. It was affecting his career prospects very directly. At least to his credit he realised this, and was taking action to deal with it. The increased discomfort of actually facing up to his skills gap, of dealing with it and following it through was, in the short term, more uncomfortable than ignoring the problem. Nevertheless it was the only way forward.

Once addressed, this would become something he could approach using new knowledge and skills, and with new confidence; ultimately, a new confidence based on the proven ability to deploy the right skills. In may be exaggerating to say that such things change our lives; it may not.

In careers, as in jobs, always tell yourself things are fine as they are, but never forget that they could be even better if they were different. Then match the thought with action.

Once upon a time (continued)

No sooner had the wolf left the lion behind, than he had a worrying thought – Wait a minute, he said to himself, just how exactly do I become a bunny rabbit? He went back, risked interrupting the lion again and said – Sorry … please … excuse me, it is, of course, a wonderful idea of yours this business of my becoming a bunny rabbit, – thank you, thank you – it solves the problem beautifully, but … but how exactly do I do that?

The lion looked, if anything, more put out than he had when first he was interrupted. But he did offer a comment nevertheless.

To be continued …

6

The way forward

Change is only another word for growth, another synonym for learning. We can all do it if we want to.

Professor Charles Handy

You have probably discovered that success in your job does not just happen. Success is not a right. You have to work at it. Those who do succeed often say that their success links directly to what they invest to achieve it (who was the golfer who said it was funny how his luck seemed to increase in direct proportion to the time he spent practicing?). That is just a reality in a dynamic and challenging world.

There are no shortcuts to any place worth going.

Beverly Sills

Amongst the things that help are:

- keeping up to date, acquiring the additional knowledge you need

- having a positive attitude to development, seeing skills as needing to be extended or added when and where necessary and taking action to upgrade your expertise

- forging the right contacts (who you know may be as important as what you know)

- analysing your results to see how things have gone, so that you utilise (and develop) the ways that helped and ditch any methodology that manifestly does not.

And more no doubt, all enabled by an attitude that seeks to maximise your effectiveness in any way possible and that aims to fit you for the tasks – however difficult – that you face in the short and long term. The higher you aim the more important all this is. Sometimes what needs to be done to take a step forward in some way is significant: perhaps time consuming or costly. That does not make it less worthwhile. Such is a development investment. As my own written work began to grow into a larger proportion of my total work portfolio some years ago, I spent some time (and much anguish!) learning how to type. I may not be the best typist in the worl#d (sic), but the action I took gave me a much greater speed and accuracy. Without the level I then acquired the profitability of my writing work would not be sufficient to make it worthwhile, despite its other advantages.

I am not suggesting that thinking in this way of investment time applied to your own work and career is a revelation; for most managers these days the premise at least is self evident, even if they do not spend as much time on it as they might wish. If you are reading a book such as this, then you are highly likely to embrace this philosophy already.

But here we have a particular opportunity. Not one, to quote an old definition, "disguised as hard work", but one that is about as straightforward to take advantage of as it is possible to be. You just need to adopt one simple and logical principle and address the fear of discomfort head on. Identify those occasions when you are putting something off or handling it dismissively just because it is awkward or difficult.

Consciously take the bull by the horns, set out to be uncomfortable and see what you can achieve.

You will in all likelihood find that, though the discomfort may be real, it is less pronounced than you had imagined, and less long lasting as well. Similarly difficult matters addressed firmly and in good time may be sorted much more easily than difficulties left to fester. Apply this to some areas and the effect may be positive, albeit undramatic. But amongst the areas at which you can direct this approach are some of real significance, those that can enhance your results generating ability in a way that will help you, your people if you manage others, and the organisation for which you work. What is needed, not least, is an attitude of positive optimism: one that assumes there is always the possibility of getting something done (even overcoming seemingly insurmountable problems – see box) if you face it and take soundly based action at the right moment.

Interlude

Thinking about being optimistic, this story always reminds me of the need to take positive action whatever the circumstances.

There is a tale from medieval times about a servant in the King's household who is condemned to life imprisonment for some small misdemeanour. Languishing in his cell, a thought about what he might do and sent a message to the King promising that, if he were released, he would work day and night and, within a year, he would teach the King's favourite horse to talk.

This amused the King, and he ordered the servant to be released to work in the Royal stables. The servant's friends were at once pleased to see him released, yet frightened for him too; after all horses do not talk, however much training they get. *"What will you do?"* they all asked. *"So much can happen in a year,"* he replied. *"I may die, the King may die, or – who knows – the horse may talk!"*

Who knows indeed; I for one hope that by the time the year was up he had thought of another ruse. So too for most of us in organisational life – the way ahead is always through taking purposeful action.

Generally speaking simple opportunities to improve performance are few indeed; or they would be taken advantage of and cease to be new opportunities. Tackling and overcoming discomfort, dealing with difficult issues and making difficult decisions, is actually a simple and available opportunity – and a powerful one. Do not waste it. Give it a try. Pick one area at which you can direct this thinking and see how you can make it work. All being well, you will emerge from the experience wanting to apply it further. The discomfort will not go away entirely, but you will find that you can deal with it – the results of so doing make it worthwhile. The ultimate habit is perhaps one of seeking out discomfort, seeing it as the trigger for action and as a sign also of an area of action that may well make a real difference to results.

It would be invidious to end the message of this book, one that leaves the ball so firmly in your court, by wishing you good luck (the preceding pages should have made clear this is the last thing you should rely on); but I wish you well. So:

Have an uncomfortable future ... it could just overcome difficulties and help you to maximise your success in job and career.

Once upon a time (concluded)

Interrupted again with a demand for more information, the lion drew himself up to his full height, ruffled his mane and said simply: As king of the jungle, I'm concerned with strategy – *how* you do it is for you to work out.

There is of, course, a moral to this story. However much advice you take, however many ideas you glean from elsewhere, taking action – appropriate and effective action – is always finally down to you. You must make a decision and you must see it through. Without such initiatives, you stagnate. In no way is there a greater truth in this than in situations where you must, logically, address difficulties head on and manage well despite being in the discomfort zone.

The rewards always make so doing well worthwhile.

Acknowledgements

As always with the management books I have written, it would be impossible to present any useful information without the stimulus of those I have worked with in many ways – clients, colleagues, contacts of all sorts – over the years. Conducting training is especially useful as the dialogue created works in both directions. I am grateful for everything than comes this way whether wittingly or unwittingly provided.

This book began with a conversation at a conference, a fellow delegate bemoaned the difficulty of making contact with others (I was sitting next to them). I noted the conversation mainly because when I asked for their business card, I was told, I'm afraid I haven't brought any. I think there was an *Oh dear* in there as well. Needless to say I do not recall their name, but thanks for setting the idea in train anyway.

So, thanks are due to many people with whom I have crossed paths along the way and who have stimulated my thinking; and to Nicholas Dale-Harris at Management Books 2000 also for his confidence in putting these thoughts into print and presenting them in such a well-designed format as part of the "90 minute" series.

For the record, the "Interlude" stories are adapted from my book *Hook Your Audience*, published by Management Pocketbooks (and the illustration is by Phil Hailstone). The full story of the tale on page 12 can be read in *Touch the Dragon* by Karen Connelly (Black Swan). *Beating the Comfort Trap* by Dr Windy Dryden and Jack Gordon (Sheldon Press) was useful in my research and, though not focused on the business world, may be a useful reference for readers.

About the author

PATRICK FORSYTH runs Touchstone Training & Consultancy, an independent firm based in the U.K. specialising in marketing consultancy and training on marketing issues, sales, and communication and management skills, including making presentations, negotiation and business writing.

He is a consultant of more than twenty years experience and was a Director of a major consulting organisation before starting his own firm in 1990. Previously he began his career in publishing, holding sales, sales management and marketing positions, subsequently working for a management institute before moving into consultancy.

His work has spanned many industries, and also many countries. He has worked in most countries in continental Europe (including eastern Europe) and also works regularly in South East Asia. In training he conducts tailored in-company courses and individual tutorials. He also conducts "public" seminars and has presented regularly for a variety of organisers including: The Institute of Management, The Chartered Institute of Marketing, The London Chamber of Commerce, The City University Business School and more specialised bodies (such as the Institute of Chartered Accountants, the Publishing Industry Training Centre and the British Council). He has also conducted such seminars for similar bodies overseas, for example the management institutes in Malaysia and Singapore.

He is the author of more than fifty successful business books. These include: *How to Write Reports and Proposals* and *How to Motivate People* (Kogan Page), and on careers, for example: *Detox Your Career* and *Manage Your Boss* (Cyan). He has titles translated into more than twenty different languages. He also writes articles (for a variety of journals such as Better Business and Professional Marketing), training materials and, more recently, for several web sites; he has written and produced corporate publications.

His work also includes a plethora of other involvements. He has acted as: a series editor for an international business publisher, training advisor for the Meetings Industry Association, advisor and presenter on two BBC television programmes on marketing and management matters, a member of the editorial board of a management journal, a communications advisor for the Civil Service in Malaysia, a mentor in the TEC small business advisory service and reviewed books for The Good Book Guide and Amazon. Recently, adding to his writing portfolio, he has had a light-hearted travel book published: this contrasts economy and first class travel, is set in South East Asia and titled, First class – at last!

He may be contacted at:

TOUCHSTONE
TRAINING AND CONSULTANCY

28 Saltcote Maltings, Heybridge, Maldon, Essex CM9 4QP United Kingdom
Telephone/fax: 01621-859300   *Email:* patrick@touchstonetc.freeserve.co.uk
marketing, sales, communications and management skills training – consultancy – business writing